The Future of Differences

For Marilyn, Judy, and John
who taught me about difference

The Future of Differences

Truth and Method in Feminist Theory

Susan J. Hekman

Polity Press

First published in 1999 by Polity Press in association with Blackwell Publishers Ltd

Editorial office:
Polity Press
65 Bridge Street
Cambridge CB2 1UR, UK

Marketing and production:
Blackwell Publishers Ltd
108 Cowley Road
Oxford OX4 1JF, UK

Published in the USA by
Blackwell Publishers Inc.
Commerce Place
350 Main Street
Malden, MA 02148, USA

ISBN 0–7456–2378–6
ISBN 0–7456–2379–4 (pbk)

A catalogue record for this book is available from the British Library.

Library of Congress Cataloging-in-Publication Data
Hekman, Susan J.
  The future of differences: truth and method in feminist theory / Susan J. Hekman.
       p.   cm.
  Includes bibliographical references and index.
  ISBN 0–7456–2378–6.—ISBN 0–7456–2379–4 (pbk.)
  1. Feminism.   2. Femininity.   3. Feminist theory.   4. Women–Identity.
I. Title
HQ1150.H45   1999   99–31167
305.42—dc21   CIP

Typeset in 10.5 on 12pt Sabon
by Kolam Information Services Pvt Ltd, Pondicherry, India

Printed in Great Britain by T. J. International, Padstow, Cornwall

This book is printed on acid-free paper.

Contents

Acknowledgments

Much of this book was written while I was serving as an associate dean in the College of Liberal Arts at the University of Texas at Arlington. I want to thank my dean, Ben Agger, for his encouragement on this project and his substantive comments on the manuscript. In 1997 I was granted a fellowship in the Research School of Social Science at the Australian National University to work on the manuscript. My stay in Canberra was stimulating intellectually as well as providing needed time to write. I am grateful to ANU and, in particular, to Barry Hindess for making this experience possible. Barry also patiently read and commented on a draft of the manuscript. Finally, I want to thank George Wright, Provost of UTA, for arranging a Faculty Development Leave in conjunction with the fellowship.

Nancy Tuana and Lynn Hankinson Nelson offered needed support at crucial points in the writing project. Alison Parker helped me to understand the concepts of feminist historians. And, as usual, Evan Anders kept me sane and prevented my most egregious mistakes. My thanks to all.

An earlier version of chapter 2 originally appeared as "Truth and Method: Feminist Standpoint Theory Revisited" in *Signs*, published by the University of Chicago Press, © 1997 by the University of Chicago. All Rights reserved. An earlier version of chapter 5 appeared in *Feminist Studies* 25(2), Summer 1999.

1

The Problem of Difference

The Other

In 1949 Simone de Beauvoir published what was to become the definitive statement of the contemporary feminist movement: *The Second Sex*. The subject of the book, de Beauvoir states in the introduction, is woman, a subject that is "irritating, especially to women; and it is not new" (1972: 13). Despite this, de Beauvoir produces a magnum opus on women: facts and myths about women; women's situation today; and, finally, the possibility of women's liberation.

"Woman," however, is not the only subject of de Beauvoir's book. Another subject, one that is central to an understanding of her exposition of woman yet is not identical to it, hovers over the analysis: the Other. Unlike "woman," the Other (always capitalized and usually italicized) does not appear on every page of the book. There are no long expositions on the qualities of the Other as there are on woman. But the Other nevertheless defines de Beauvoir's explanation of "woman" at every crucial juncture. She first asserts that "The category of the *Other* is as primordial as consciousness itself" (1972: 16). "Otherness is a fundamental category of human thought. Thus it is that no group even sets itself up as the One without at once setting up the Other over against itself" (1972: 17). It is de Beauvoir's discussion of the Other that explains her apparently contradictory statement at the beginning of the book that masculine and feminine are not symmetrical terms, because the masculine is both the positive and the neutral in this dichotomy (1972: 15). Men, who define themselves in opposition to women, are both "the One," the positive opposed to the negative pole of "the Other" (women), and, at the same time, the neutral standard that defines humanness itself. Woman is, thus, both a negative and a lack – both something that, by opposing "the One," is necessary for its definition and at the same time nothing at all, because she fails to measure up to the standard defined by "the One."

The story that de Beauvoir wants to tell about the Other is, apparently, very simple: women must overcome their otherness relative to men, that is, their lack and negativity; this overcoming is the means of their liberation. Despite the simplicity of this message, however, it is obvious from the outset that de Beauvoir's understanding of the Other raises difficult if not insuperable epistemological difficulties for her story. Her premise is that otherness is as primordial as consciousness itself, that it is a necessary condition of all human thought and knowledge. Specifically, it is necessary for the definition of subjectivity. "The One," the acting human subject, must define himself in terms of the Other in order to achieve subjectivity. It is obvious from this that the Otherness of women will, at the very least, be difficult to overcome. In the course of her analysis, de Beauvoir lays out the difficulties in some detail. The first is that women are complicit in the maintenance of their status as "Other": "If woman seems to be the inessential which never becomes the essential, it is because she herself fails to bring about this change.... The division of the sexes is a biological fact, not an event in human history. Male and female stand opposed within a primordial *Mitsein*, and woman has not broken it" (1972: 19). The reason for this complicity, de Beauvoir claims, is that women derive advantages from their status: "To decline to be the Other, to refuse to be a party to the deal – this would be for women to renounce all the advantages conferred upon them by their alliance with the superior caste" (1972: 21).

De Beauvoir also outlines a deeper problem that plagues the One/Other relationship, a problem rooted in epistemology: "Here is to be found the basic trait of woman: she is the Other in a totality of which the two components are necessary to one another" (1972: 20). De Beauvoir details the results of this epistemological coupling of One and Other in the course of the book. The most telling passage on the Other is found in a chapter on "Dreams, Fears, Idols." In the context of a discussion of Kierkegaard, de Beauvoir states:

For if woman is not the only *Other*, it remains none the less true that she is always defined as the Other. And her ambiguity is just that of the concept of the Other: it is that of the human situation in so far as it is defined in its relation with the Other. As I have already said, the Other is Evil; but being necessary to the Good, it turns into the Good; through it I attain to the Whole, but it also separates me therefrom; it is the gateway to the infinite and the measure of my finite nature. (1972: 175)

To label woman's position in the One/Other relationship "ambiguous" distorts the seriousness of the epistemological problem that de Beauvoir has described.[1] By her account, woman's otherness defines her as a necessary tool for the attainment of man's transcendence, his realization of his true subjectivity. Without the juxtaposition of the Other to his One, man is indefinable; this juxtaposition is the necessary condition of his knowledge of self and the world. What this entails for the subjectivity of women, however, is less clear. On one hand, woman, de Beauvoir states, "appears as the *privileged Other*, through whom the subject fulfills himself: one of the measures of man, his counterbalance, his salvation, his adventure, his happiness" (1972: 278). As Other, then, woman is not a full subject herself, but a means to the subjectivity of man. But de Beauvoir also makes it clear that this Other status cannot be reinterpreted and transformed into a vehicle for woman's full subjectivity. She states:

In sexuality and maternity woman as subject can claim autonomy; but to be a 'true woman' she must accept herself as the Other. The men of today show a certain duplicity of attitude which is painfully lacerating to women; they are willing on the whole to accept woman as a fellow being, an equal; but they still require her to remain the inessential. (1972: 291)

In this passage de Beauvoir introduces the theme that becomes her blueprint for the liberation of woman: accepting woman as a fellow being, an equal. In the conclusion to the book she states that "The quarrel [between men and women] will go on as long as men and women fail to recognize each other as equals; that is to say, as long as femininity is perpetuated as such" (1972: 727–8). To effect this change, "social evolution" is necessary that will result in girls being brought up with the same expectations as boys (1972: 734–5). The problems of women can be surmounted in the future, she argues, "when they are regarded in new perspectives" (1972: 736). If men and women mutually recognize each other as subjects, "each will yet remain for the Other an *Other*. The reciprocity of their relations will not do away with the miracles – desire, possession, love, dream, adventure – worked by the division of human beings into two separate categories" (1972: 740). And, finally,

> when we abolish the slavery of half of humanity, then the 'division' of humanity will reveal its genuine significance and the human couple will find its true form.... To gain the supreme victory, it is necessary for one thing, that by and through their natural differentiation men and women unequivocally affirm their brotherhood. (1972: 741)

Let's look at this conclusion from an epistemological perspective. First, a strict equality between men and women is impossible within the One/Other relationship. The epistemological strictures of the One/Other dichotomy demand the inequality of these two elements. To attain full subjectivity, then, men and, presumably, women as well must attain the status of the One, a status defined in terms of the ability to transcend the immanence of life, achieve autonomy, and embrace freedom. In order to be a One, the subject must define him or herself in contrast to an Other who embodies the opposite of these qualities: immanence and dependence. This juxtaposition works quite well, as de Beauvoir has shown, when the One is masculine and the Other feminine. It becomes confused, however, when, as de Beauvoir proposes, men and women reciprocate the One/Other statuses. As de Beauvoir envisions it, women would become, alternately, the Other to men's One and the One to men's Other; men would alternate these statuses as well. The result, de Beauvoir hopes, would be full subjectivity for both sexes.

The question is whether such an alternation would work. First, men would have to be willing to assume the status of Other, at least on a temporary basis. But there is little motivation for them to do so, given the definitions of the two statuses. De Beauvoir paints a dismal picture of Otherness: mired in immanence, subservience to the One who defines the standard of subjectivity to be achieved, dependence rather than autonomy. Men, having attained the status of the One, would have little incentive to renounce this status, particularly when the alternative is the Other, a status that is both a negative and a necessary element of their own transcendence. Second, de Beauvoir's scheme requires that women assume the status of the One, transcend their immanence and embrace their freedom. To accomplish this, women must embrace all the qualities that define the One and, most importantly, juxtaposition to a subservient but necessary Other.

It is at this point that the weakness of de Beauvoir's formula becomes clear. The qualities of the One are gendered masculine: transcendence, freedom, autonomy. In order to become the One, woman must not only definitively renounce her femininity and all the qualities that entails; she must also embrace the distinctively masculine qualities that define the One. De Beauvoir is very clear about this: the standard of subjectivity remains these masculine qualities. It follows that woman will always be a second-class citizen in the realm of the One, because these qualities are alien to her. Further complicating woman's situation is the necessity of convincing man to take on the unsavory role of Other that she has renounced. In addition to the obvious liabilities of this role, it is also gendered feminine. Thus man would find the role of the Other as alien as woman finds the role of the One.

If all this sounds excessively convoluted and even a bit absurd, it is because de Beauvoir is attempting an epistemological impossibility. What de Beauvoir's analysis reveals, although she refuses to admit it, is that the category of the One is inherently and not incidentally masculine, just as the category of the Other is inherently feminine. Her efforts to argue for the equality of women while staying within the parameters of this dichotomy ultimately founder on the epistemological necessity defined by the dichotomy. Men cannot and have no incentive to become the Other to woman's One. Conversely, women cannot become the One because, ultimately, the definition excludes her.

The question remains, however, why de Beauvoir comes to a conclusion that is, at best, both banal and logically unrelated to her previous analysis. De Beauvoir abandons the logic of her insightful analysis of the masculine/feminine relationship to conclude with an admonition that she has shown to be impossible: woman should be respected as man's equal. The only explanation for this resolution is that de Beauvoir has painstakingly described an insuperable epistemological dilemma and, lacking an exit from that dilemma, has retreated to platitudes that sidestep it.

The broad outlines of what de Beauvoir is arguing in *The Second Sex* are not, of course, unique. She is not the only one to argue that the dominant pattern in Western thought has been dualistic, and that these dualisms are both hierarchical and gendered.[2] But de Beauvoir's analysis of the One/Other dualism is uniquely insightful. Her emphasis on both the necessity and the asymmetry of this duality places it in a new light. Although other feminists calling for the liberation of women, most notably Wollstonecraft and Mill, had analyzed this dualism and argued that women can attain equality with men, de Beauvoir's analysis reveals that woman is trapped in this dualistic epistemology. De Beauvoir's argument that woman represents both the opposite of the active, agentic male subject and the definition of the absence of subjectivity makes the conception of a "liberated" feminine subject an epistemological impossibility. Furthermore, de Beauvoir's philosophical rigor combined with her emphasis on the "liberation" of women highlights the epistemological difficulty of escaping from the One/Other dualism. Her logic leads her to conclude that there is no escape from the dualism; yet, as an advocate of "women's liberation," she cannot accept this conclusion. The inconsistent resolution she offers thus highlights the impossibility of the dilemma she so carefully details.

The aim of this book is to examine the problem of difference in feminist theory. I begin that examination with de Beauvoir, most obviously, because her work is path breaking; it set the agenda for feminist theory for decades. But there is also a less obvious reason for beginning with de Beauvoir: the philosophical rigor of her work reveals why that agenda ultimately fails. De Beauvoir provides a clear outline of the strategies that are open to women seeking "liberation" from the dualisms that structure patriarchy. The first strategy is to become the One, to abandon the status of Other and the negativity and lack that it entails. The second is to imbue the Other with the autonomy of subjectivity and thus elevate it to equality with the One. De Beauvoir argues that feminists should pursue the first strategy. Conversely, her rejection of the second strategy, her almost obsessive devaluation of the feminine, has become legendary. But the logic of de Beauvoir's analysis just as clearly indicates that neither strategy can succeed. There are two conclusions to *The Second Sex*: the political admonition to seek the equality of women and the philosophical conclusion that this goal is impossible.

The evolution of feminist theory over the next four decades can be interpreted as the process of working out the possibilities of the two strategies that de Beauvoir outlines, culminating in the conclusion that both are epistemologically bankrupt. This evolution was, of course, due in large part to the fact that the epistemology that informs de Beauvoir's analysis was not of her invention: the gendered dichotomy she explicates is central to the modernist tradition from which she writes. It is no surprise, then, that neither she nor the succeeding generations of feminists were willing to abandon it. Reading de Beauvoir today, it seems obvious why both strategies failed. As both the first and then the second strategies were being pursued, however, there were compelling reasons why each, in turn, appeared to be the best option for the feminist movement.

Much has been written about what might be called "the difference shift" in feminist theory. The outlines of that history are now clear: first, the effort to erase the differences between men and women; second, the emphasis on those differences and the valorization of the feminine; third, the exploration of differences among women. I am going to begin my analysis of the problem of difference in feminist theory by sketching the outlines of this history, for several reasons. First, I think that the epistemological significance of the progression has not been fully appreciated by contemporary feminists. Along with many others, I argue that, epistemologically, the first and second strategies are two sides of the same coin; both spell defeat for the effort to "liberate" women. But I also argue that it was the process of exploring these two strategies that led feminists to what is, in Althusser's metaphor, a new continent of thought. In other words, the failure to make sense out of difference led feminists to differences. As a consequence of that move, feminism has been and continues to be, on the forefront of the paradigm shift that characterizes late twentieth-century thought, the shift from foundational to anti-foundational thought.

My second reason is that I think it is imperative that feminists get on with the task of devising a theory and method for differences. If, as I am arguing, the exploration of differences defines a new epistemological space, then feminism needs a new definition of truth and method to operate in that space. In the era of differences new problems arise that demand new solutions. How can we work for the liberation of women when the general category of "woman" is a problematic concept? What truth does our method seek if truths are multiple and perspectival? It is my contention that developing a new understanding of truth and method is the major challenge facing contemporary feminism. A better understanding of the epistemology of difference in feminist theory is a necessary first step in meeting that challenge.

From erasure to emphasis

De Beauvoir was not the first feminist to advocate what I am calling the first strategy – the erasure of difference and the pursuit of equality. Previous advocates of women's liberation had, like de Beauvoir, also based their argument for the equality of women on the erasure of difference. What sets de Beauvoir's account apart, however, is the radical extreme to which she takes this argument. In her attempt to erase difference, she takes on the aspect of femininity that is both its defining feature and its most valorized attribute: maternity.

A comparison between de Beauvoir's position in *The Second Sex* and a previous attempt to erase difference, John Stuart Mill's *The Subjection of Women* ([1869]1971), reveals the distinctiveness of her position. The theme of Mill's book, like that of de Beauvoir's, is apparently very straightforward: women are equal to men and thus must be granted equal rights. But even a casual examination of the book reveals the ambiguity of Mill's argument for the equality of women and throws serious doubt on the possibility or even the desirability of attaining this goal. Mill spends a great deal of time agonizing over the question of whether men and women have different natures, ultimately concluding that, under present conditions, it is impossible to tell. Anticipating the subsequent rise of a social constructionist position, he argues that what we define as the "nature" of men and women is the result of social and cultural forces, not necessarily that of innate differences. But his most revealing argument comes in his discussion of rationality. Mill concedes that women's deficiency in rationality is a product of their inferior education and argues that man's capacity for rational abstraction is the cause of the intellectual advancements of mankind. He does not, however, adopt the obvious conclusion to this argument: that women embrace man's style of rationality and abandon the womanly style. Rather, he argues that

> it remains to be shown whether this inclusive working of a part of the mind, this absorption of the whole thinking faculty on a single subject and concentration of it on a single work is the normal and healthful condition of the human faculties, even for speculative uses. ([1869]1971: 502)

What Mill suggests instead is a thesis that enjoyed much popularity in the nineteenth century: complementarity. The masculine capacity for sustained abstract thought, he claims, should be complemented by woman's more practical, intuitive style. Thus, in this crucial area Mill shies away from a radical advocacy of the erasure of difference. He wants to preserve some of the differences between men and women while at the same time arguing for their equality. Significantly, it is the traditional division of labor between men and women that he wants to preserve. That men engage in tasks requiring muscular exertion and women concern themselves with the fine arts is, he claims, "natural" and "healthy" (Mill and Mill 1970: 77). And, although he does not state it explicitly, Mill assumes that the most natural role for women is that of wife and mother, a role that most women will "choose" over other occupations ([1869]1971: 484). Ultimately, Mill does not want to erase the differences between men and women but, rather, to retain certain "feminine" traits, a move that precludes the equality he claims to seek.[3]

De Beauvoir's argument for the erasure of difference exhibits no such ambiguity. She rejects the complementarity thesis simply because she sees no advantages to the feminine side of the masculine/feminine dichotomy. What is distinctive about de Beauvoir's argument is that her denigration of the feminine extends to what has seemed to both the advocates and the opponents of feminism to be its essence: maternity. Even the most enthusiastic proponents of the equality of men and women had shied away from arguing for erasing the presumably sexual difference embodied in the role of maternity. Maternity was seen as both the "natural," biological role of women and the embodiment of all the positive values associated with the feminine. De Beauvoir rejects both these assumptions. She identifies maternity as *the* obstacle to the equality of women and, with her characteristic logical rigor, argues that this difference, above all others, must be erased.

De Beauvoir insures that none of her readers miss the point of her argument by beginning her section on "The Mother" with a long discussion of abortion. Her conclusion is that "contraception and legal abortion would permit woman to undertake her maternities in freedom" (1972: 510). She moves from this to her now infamous condemnation of the female body and its functions. Women who are continually pregnant, she states, are "fertile organisms, like fowl with high egg-production. And they seek eagerly to sacrifice their liberty of action to the function of their flesh: it seems to them that their existence is tranquilly justified in the passive fecundity of their bodies" (1972: 513).

Few feminists had been quite so scathing in their denunciation of the sacred role of motherhood. De Beauvoir's unqualified rejection of the female body has led many feminists to reject her work in its entirety. But there is an important epistemological lesson in de Beauvoir's position that is significant for an understanding of the history of difference. It follows from her rejection of all things female that any attempt on the part of women to employ their immanence as

fleshly mothers to achieve the transcendence that alone defines true
subjectivity is doomed to failure:

> If the flesh is purely passive and inert, it cannot embody transcendence
> even in degraded form; it is sluggish and tiresome; but when
> the reproductive process begins, the flesh becomes root- stock, source,
> and blossom, it assumes transcendence, a stirring towards the future,
> the while it remains a gross and present reality.... With her ego
> surrendered, alienated in her body and in her social dignity, the mother
> enjoys the comforting illusion of feeling that she is a human being *in
> herself a value.*
> But this is only an illusion. (1972: 513)

De Beauvoir counters:

> Creative acts originating in liberty establish the object as value and
> give it the quality of the essential; whereas the child in the maternal
> body is not thus justified; it is still only a gratuitous cellular growth, a
> brute fact of nature as contingent on circumstances as death and
> corresponding philosophically with it. (1972: 514)

In these passages de Beauvoir denies the underlying premise of the
second strategy: that the realm of the feminine can provide the basis
for the attainment of subjectivity. She argues that because the feminine is the realm of the immanent and of death, it is an impediment
rather than a means to transcendence. Further, by attacking the locus
of the apparently irreducible biological difference between men and
women – maternity – de Beauvoir defines the extreme pole in the
argument for the erasure of difference, its logically inescapable conclusion. Far from valorizing maternity, she imagines a society in
which the role of motherhood is freely chosen and, when undertaken,
reduced to a minimum. Her ideal is a society in which children would
be "largely taken in charge by the community" thus freeing the
mother for the pursuit of a career (1972: 540).

In one sense, de Beauvoir should be applauded for her philosophical rigor. She realizes, as previous feminists had not, that if we argue
for the erasure of difference as the means to the equality of the sexes,
then we must abandon our sentimental attachment to motherhood
and erase this difference as well. But the philosophical rigor of de
Beauvoir's argument about difference leads her to the contradiction
that I noted above. The erasure of difference in maternity is a vital
link in the argument that leads to de Beauvoir's conclusion: that
women and men be treated equally and affirm their "brotherhood."

It is only by erasing this crucial and significant difference that the full equality of women can be achieved. But erasing this final difference entails the erasure of the One/Other distinction that, de Beauvoir has also argued, is both logically and existentially necessary to the definition of human subjectivity. Another way of putting this is that the logic of her difference argument leads to a contradiction in her subjectivity argument: if difference is erased, then subjectivity cannot be defined.

The contradictions inherent in de Beauvoir's approach to difference and subjectivity play themselves out in the history of feminist theory in the succeeding decades. Tracing feminists' treatment of maternity in these decades highlights the effects of those contradictions. De Beauvoir's radical approach to maternity is the model for a book that marks a turning point in feminist theory: Shulamith Firestone's *The Dialectic of Sex* (1970). Firestone fills out the outline of radical equality that de Beauvoir only sketches in *The Second Sex*. She is acutely aware of the radical nature of her approach; in fact, she exults in it. Feminist change, Firestone declares, is the most revolutionary, because it attacks not just culture, but nature itself. The revolt of the underclass of women requires their seizure of control of reproduction. Such a seizure would entail that genital conditions would no longer matter; the reproduction of the species by one sex for the benefit of both would be replaced by artificial reproduction in which children would be born to both sexes equally (1970: 11–12). As a result, Firestone claims, "The tyranny of the biological family would be broken" (1970: 12).

Firestone's polemic advances the argument for the erasure of difference on several fronts. First, it defines the feminist revolution as the most radical revolution possible – more so than Marx's understanding of the proletarian revolution to which Firestone frequently compares it: "The sexual-reproductive organization of society always furnishes the real basis, starting from which we can alone work out the ultimate explanation of the whole superstructure of economic, juridical and political institutions as well as of the religious, philosophical and other ideas of a given historical period" (1970: 14). Second, Firestone takes de Beauvoir's negative portrayal of maternity to a further extreme by arguing that "The heart of women's oppression is her childbearing and childrearing roles" (1970: 81). "Pregnancy," Firestone claims, "is barbaric" (1970: 226). Women do "damage" to their children in their childrearing practice. Third, Firestone outlines what the world would look like if this final difference between men and women were erased. She advocates a utopia of "cybernetic socialism," contractual households, and complete freedom for women and children. Childbearing would be "taken over by technology," and the concept of childhood itself would be abolished (1970: 270–1). Even more clearly than *The Second Sex*, *The Dialectic of Sex* reveals the logical consequences of the argument for the erasure of difference. Firestone pursues the logic of this argument with admirable rigor, describing a society without mothers or even children. That the conclusions she derives are unappealing even to other feminists is not due to faulty logic; it is a consequence of the basic premises of the argument.

It is tempting to argue that what Firestone accomplished in *The Dialectic of Sex* was the *reductio ad absurdum* of the erasure of difference and, thus, that the subsequent shift in feminist theory from the erasure to the emphasis on difference was inevitable. Whether or not this is so, it is the case that a sea change occurred in feminist theory in the 1980s that entailed the abandonment of what I am calling the first strategy and the adoption of the second strategy. I trace this change by analyzing two pairs of books that address the pivotal issue of maternity; in each pair one of the books represents the first strategy, one the second. This analysis has several purposes. It reveals the contrasts between the two strategies on this issue, but it shows that there are continuities as well. Further, it shows that elements of the second strategy reveal the beginnings of a paradigm shift in feminist theory on the subject of difference that will lead from difference to differences.

The first pair of books consists of Firestone's *The Dialectic of Sex* and Mary O'Brien's *The Politics of Reproduction* (1981). No more need be said about the conformity of Firestone to the first strategy. O'Brien's book, by contrast, is an almost perfect example of the second strategy. Despite her radical rejection of the first strategy, however, O'Brien's approach shares elements of that strategy. Like Firestone and, before her, de Beauvoir, O'Brien defines motherhood and reproduction as central to the differences between men and women and to the oppression of women. Also like Firestone and de Beauvoir, O'Brien operates according to a strict binary: men versus women. Differences within these categories are not explored. But that O'Brien is also moving into different territory is clear from the outset. O'Brien's first chapter is labeled "The Dialectics of Reproduction," explicitly evoking Firestone's title. O'Brien's aim is to highlight the contrast between her text and Firestone's. For O'Brien reproduction is a process, an institution, a social phenomenon; sex, by contrast, is a biological fact. This shift is of central importance.

Although feminists since Wollstonecraft had been aware of the role of social conditioning in the oppression of women, this awareness now moves to center stage. Once the differences between men and women are defined as primarily the result of social processes, and these social processes are defined as creating different "realities" for men and women, two changes occur. First, the malleability of these processes becomes increasingly evident. Biology cannot be changed, but socialization can. The focus of feminist interest thus becomes attempts to change the socialization process. Second, the emphasis on social processes leads to an emphasis on diversity. Clearly, social processes, unlike sex, come in more than two varieties. If social processes create different realities, then it must be the case that they create more than just two, masculine or feminine. The way is thus open for a discussion of multiple social realities.

O'Brien is not ready, however, to plunge into an examination of the differences within the categories of masculine and feminine. But, unlike the proponents of the first strategy, she is ready to define the "masculine experience" as a "conception of reality" and to classify it as deficient. Her goal in the book is to ask what it is about the masculine experience that structures conceptions of reality and, further, what will enable women to develop a feminist theory that can "explore the reality of being female" (1981: 6). For O'Brien, this exploration must start with the quintessentially feminine experience: reproduction. It is in this aspect of her theory that O'Brien takes on de Beauvoir most directly. She insists that feminists must create their own rules of rational discourse, not merely mimic those of men: "De Beauvoir's female existent simply cries 'Me, too!' She has been shown by men the possibility of freedom and wants it, but has not, like Hegel's slave, discovered the possibility for herself" (1981: 71). O'Brien notes that Firestone extends de Beauvoir's insight to its logical conclusion: the transcendence of biology (1981: 78). O'Brien's alternative is a phrase that will become emblematic of the second strategy: the standpoint of women.

O'Brien is one of the strongest advocates of the second strategy that de Beauvoir so thoroughly condemned: achieving transcendence through the feminine, not the masculine. Freedom for women, O'Brien insists, must not be an act that imitates men but, rather, a confrontation and struggle with masculine otherness (1981: 73). To accomplish this women must develop their own theory, their own rules, of rational discourse. For O'Brien the central element of this project is developing a philosophy of birth rooted in women's reality. She explicates in detail precisely what de Beauvoir claimed was impossible: the definition of full subjectivity within the feminine sphere.[4]

A similar shift in the conception of difference is played out in the second pair of contrasting books: Nancy Chodorow's *The Reproduction of Mothering* (1978) and Sara Ruddick's *Maternal Thinking* (1989). The first sentence of *The Reproduction of Mothering* states an obvious yet vastly significant fact: "women mother." The goal of Chodorow's book is to explore the far-reaching implications of this social phenomenon. Reading Chodorow from the perspective of the 1990s it is easy to place her in the "maternal thinking" camp that valorizes the caring function of mothers. But from a strictly epistemological perspective this is not an accurate reading of her work. Like de Beauvoir, Chodorow sees women's mothering as a problem requiring a solution and, further, that this solution entails the erasure of the uniquely feminine characteristics of this role.

Chodorow's interpretation of the first sentence of her book sets the tone for her subsequent argument: women's mothering is a problem to be explored. From the outset, Chodorow approaches mothering as a social rather than a biological phenomenon. She analyzes how this phenomenon came about, what social and political results it has produced, and, significantly, how the practice can be changed. She quickly dispenses with biology as a "cause" of exclusively feminine mothering and moves on to psychoanalysis as an explanatory tool. Rejecting much previous psychoanalytic theory because it assumes a biological necessity for women's mothering, Chodorow turns instead to socially based theories. Object-relations theory, finally, offers her the perspective that she is seeking to explain the differences between men and women. She concludes: "These outcomes, like more traditional Oedipal outcomes, arise from the asymmetrical organization of parenting, with the Mother's role as primary parent and the father's typically greater remoteness and his investment in socialization especially in areas concerned with gender-typing" (1978: 166).

The story that Chodorow tells is by now a very familiar one: women's mothering produces women who are good at relationships and bad at autonomy and the opposite configuration in men. But, far from arguing that women's mothering is a positive force that can be utilized to transform an alienated masculine world, Chodorow, like de Beauvoir, wants instead to transform the world by erasing the difference she has described. The present social organization of parenting, she argues, produces sexual inequality; and it follows that "It is politically and socially important to confront this organization of parenting" (1978: 214). The goal of the solution that Chodorow proposes, equally shared primary parenting, is to eliminate this inequality. The elimination of exclusive female mothering, she concludes, would be a "tremendous social advance" (1978: 219).

Chodorow is not as hard on mothers as de Beauvoir. She concedes that "many mothers and infants are mutually gratified through their relationship and many mothers enjoy taking care of their infants" (1978: 86). Unlike de Beauvoir, Chodorow wants to combine the good aspects of masculinity and femininity. The equal parenting she recommends would, she hopes, leave both genders with the positive aspects of the gender, but without the "destructive extremes" (1978: 218). But these are scattered remarks in a book that, overall, defines mothering as a problem. Despite her conformity to the epistemology of the first strategy, however, Chodorow, like O'Brien, introduces a new and eventually highly significant change: an emphasis on socialization rather than biology. While de Beauvoir and Firestone were not unaware of social factors, their emphasis was on biology. Chodorow shifts this emphasis by focusing almost exclusively on socialization. She thus opens up the possibility for a new approach to difference although she herself does not adopt that approach.

That Sara Ruddick's approach to mothering is very different is evident from the first pages of *Maternal Thinking*. Ruddick begins with an account of what she identifies as her "love affair" with "Reason" and her gradual disenchantment with the concept. She concludes: "Reason, at least as Western philosophers had imagined Him, was infected by – and contributed to – the pervasive disrespect for women's minds and lives from which I suffered. For a woman to love Reason was to risk both self-contempt and a self-alienating misogyny" (1989: 4–5). She definitively rejects de Beauvoir's first strategy, the erasure of difference, as fundamentally flawed: "We have learned from confronting racism and sexual bigotry that we cannot make our differences disappear. To deny the different relations of women and men to human birth founds the entire egalitarian project on an illusion" (1989: 49). Ruddick's counter is that mothers must think, and this is a form of reasoning that, although different from "Reason," is nevertheless valid. The thesis of Ruddick's book is that women's activity of mothering provides principles that can be used to formulate a feminist maternal peace politics. Her complex argument revolves around questioning and redefining "reason" as it has been known in Western philosophy.

Ruddick's rejection of "Reason" and her valorization of women's different form of reasoning places her argument solidly in the second strategy camp. But Ruddick's work occupies a significant place in the feminist epistemology of difference in that it also moves beyond the second strategy in a fundamental respect: questioning the absolutism of the dichotomous concept of difference. At the very outset Ruddick asserts that she is not seeking a "total and inclusive narrative of all true statements," because no such narrative exists (1989: 13). The "maternal thinking" that she seeks is, rather, a "practicalist view," thinking that arises from and is tested against practices. She thus makes it clear that she is neither seeking the truth of masculine reason nor substituting a feminist reason/truth for it. Ruddick's departure from the strict masculine/feminine dichotomy is reinforced by her insistence that both men and women can be "mothers." Although Ruddick makes a passionate case for maternal thinking, she significantly qualifies her argument by insisting that this ethical position has no exclusive claim to truth. She describes maternal thinking as "only one discipline among others" (1989: 127). Significantly, she does not shy away from the epistemological consequences of her position. Instead, she asserts that feminism itself challenges the notion of aperspectivity and universality (1989: 128). Instead of asserting the "truth" of maternal thinking, she asserts only that "thoughtful people" will be able to "generalize the potentiality made available by the activity of women," caring labor, to society as a whole (1989: 132).

The uniqueness of Ruddick's position in the feminist discussion of difference is that although she has come to represent the epitome of what I am calling the second strategy, her epistemology effectively deconstructs this strategy and points the way to a third, quite different strategy. Epistemologically, the first and second strategies are mirror images of each other; their similarities outweigh their differences. Both presuppose essential or culturally imposed differences between men and women; both presuppose a hierarchy of those differences; and both ignore differences within the two categories. The two strategies differ only in their valuations of the two sides of the dichotomy. The first strategy values the masculine side and wants to turn women into men; the second values the feminine side and argues for the superiority of feminine values. Another way of putting this is that in the first strategy the feminine is seen as a deficiency, and thus as something to be erased and subsumed under the masculine. In the second strategy the feminine is seen as an asset, and thus must be emphasized and valorized. Ruddick effectively deconstructs this neat dichotomy by denying that either side possesses truth. Just as the movement from biological to social difference paved the way from the first to the second strategy, so Ruddick's deconstruction paves the way for the paradigm shift that characterizes subsequent feminist treatments of difference.

From difference to differences

In 1979 Barnard College sponsored a conference entitled "The Scholar and the Feminist VI: The Future of Difference." The participants at the conference reflected on what I am calling the shift from the first to the second strategy – from the erasure to the emphasis on difference (Eisenstein and Jardine 1980). In her introduction to the volume that emerged from the conference, Hester Eisenstein attributes the change to women's realization in the 1970s that women's difference from men was a source of enrichment, not a tool of oppression (Eisenstein 1980: xviii). In the 1980s many feminists concurred with this assessment. They defined the emphasis on and valorization of the feminine as a positive and necessary step for the feminist movement. But, particularly as the decade progressed, some feminists began to raise questions about the wisdom of this shift. Iris Young, for example, cautions that emphasizing the superiority of the feminine can be "quieting and accommodating to official powers" (1985: 173). In 1982 Carol Gilligan published *In a Different Voice*, the book that quickly came to be interpreted as the definitive statement of the second strategy.[5] Despite the popularity of Gilligan's book, however, serious questions about the wisdom of promoting the "different voice" were raised. Echoing Young's fears, Claudia Card labeled Gilligan's position "conservative," because it promotes the revival of traditional, middle-class conceptions of femininity (1991: 17). Genevieve Lloyd put this position most bluntly in her statement that glorifying female difference may doom women to "repeat some of the sadder subplots of the history of western thought" (1984: 105).

These questions are a function of the epistemological similarity between the first and second strategies. Although the second strategy reversed the hierarchy of the first strategy, it shares important epistemological assumptions with it: both strategies assume that the differences between men and women are monolithic and hierarchical, that qualities are either masculine *or* feminine, either superior *or* inferior. Assuming the superiority of masculine qualities created serious problems for the first strategy. But assuming the superiority of the feminine created equally difficult problems for the second strategy. Once again, Genevieve Lloyd defined the difficulty: embodied femaleness cannot be both the source of our oppression and the means of its transcendence (1984: 105). The dichotomy that informs both the first and the second strategies demands one right answer to the question of how liberation is to be achieved. Questions about the second strategy began to reveal that either/or choices were insufficient for feminist epistemology, that feminist discussions must move beyond these strict dichotomies.

The emphasis on the social/discursive character of difference that was a springboard for the shift from the first to the second strategy also provided the impetus for defining a new epistemological space in feminist theory: the exploration of differences. As feminists began to explore the social/discursive construction of sexual difference, they discovered that a wide array of differences were socially and discursively constituted, and that to accommodate these differences, new strategies were necessary. What was not clear at the outset, however, was that the emphasis on differences created a set of problems that demanded a new epistemology and methodology for feminist theory and practice.

The problem that first occupied the attention of feminist theorists who explored the issue of differences was that of subjectivity and the closely connected issue of agency.[6] The One/Other epistemology presupposes an agentic, Cartesian subject that is the source of knowledge. Although the feminists who espoused the second strategy rejected the masculine subject of this tradition, they remained within its epistemological space by espousing the feminine subject as its equal and opposite. Central to both these conceptions is the assumption that the subject is defined by an essential core and, most importantly, that differences are not constitutive of subjectivity. An epistemology of differences, however, must develop a conception of subjectivity that defines differences as constitutive rather than marginal. The defining feature of the Cartesian subject is the stability of its identity: it assumes a universal human essence. By contrast, the subject of differences is unstable – its identity varies according to an array of differences, only one of which is gender. The challenge is to define the identity of this subject without losing coherence. Thus, as Kathy Ferguson argues, we must conceive of subjectivity as "mobile – temporal, relational and shifting, yet enduring, ambiguous, messy and multiple" (1993: 154). The Cartesian subject, furthermore, is an agentic subject, a subject that is the undisputed author of its actions. A non-Cartesian definition of the subject demands a new conception of agency that does not presuppose an autonomous acting subject. Feminists realized that they could not abandon agency, yet needed to redefine it radically to match the subject of differences.[7]

That this issue is still a highly contentious one in feminism is evidenced by Marilyn Frye's recent article in *Signs* (1996). With her characteristic precision, Frye outlines exactly what is implicit in the epistemology of the One/Other, or, as she puts it, A/not A. The problem with the A/not A distinction is that within the not A category, historically that of women, distinctions are obliterated – all elements in the category are equally not A. What we need, she claims, is a positive category that is self-supporting rather than dependent on negation. A positive category, she argues, is "a plurality with internal structure whose elements are differentiated and differentiable and are in a significant variety of relations with each other and that is, by virtue of this structure, coalesced as a distinguishable 'something'" (1996: 1002). It is a category, in short, that necessarily depends on difference rather than sameness.

Frye not only offers an insightful analysis of the strictures imposed by the A/not A (One/Other) epistemology, she also reveals the disquiet that feminists feel with regard to abandoning the concept of subjectivity that this epistemology entails. Abandoning the One/Other epistemology that has informed feminist thought since de Beauvoir, not to mention modernity itself, poses daunting questions. In her account Frye is trying to answer two of these questions: How can we conceive of a subject apart from the either/or categories of the Cartesian subject? How can we give this subject agency? These and related questions are being widely discussed by feminists in the 1990s. But little has been resolved in these discussions other than the agreement that feminism requires a new conception of subjectivity. There is no agreement on the parameters of that subjectivity, or how a non-Cartesian agency can be defined.[8]

One way of characterizing this situation is that feminists are uncomfortable in a radically new epistemology – they don't, in a sense, know their way about. Another aspect of this dis-ease is the realm of politics. The politics spawned by modernist epistemology is a politics of Cartesian, agentic subjects pursuing goals such as freedom, emancipation, and rights. Feminist political action in the 1960s and 1970s conformed neatly to this model. Pursuing the first strategy, women entered the political world with the aspiration of becoming men's equals and thus to achieve the goal of "women's liberation." As the second strategy gained ascendancy in the 1980s, many feminists abandoned this definition of feminist politics in favor of "maternal politics" – acting as embodied women in the political world and pursuing specifically feminine goals. Despite their differences, however, these strategies were similar in that they presupposed the category of "Woman" and pursued a better life for those falling into that category.

In the 1990s, however, many feminists have begun to define feminist politics in terms of the "politics of difference." Discussions around the politics of difference highlight both the advantages of the rejection of the Cartesian subject and the problems it generates. The politics of difference "rejects false universalisms and homogeneous totalisms"; it "trashes the monolithic and homogeneous in the name of diversity, multiplicity" (West 1994: 78, 65). In the politics of difference, marginalized agents enter the political world retaining rather than shedding their identity. There are significant advantages to this approach. The myth of the universal political actor is exploded; differences among political actors are recognized as a constitutive part of political action. But the problems created by the politics of difference are just as significant. How can these different political identities come together in a political movement? What will be the basis for political unity if we question the basis of commonality? What West calls "the universalisms and homogeneous totalisms" of modernist politics constitute that politics. The politics of difference demands not just a different political strategy, but an epistemology that redefines both political action and the political actor.

Feminists and other advocates of the politics of difference have attempted to answer these questions. Most advocate some form of coalition politics (Laclau and Mouffe 1985, Young 1990, Coles 1996). The key question in all these arguments is what constitutes the basis for this coalition – what unifying ethic or theme holds the coalition together. Various ethics have been suggested. Romand Coles suggests an "ethic of receptive generosity" that will prevent the disintegration of the politics of difference (1996: 387). Iris Young suggests a "radically pluralist participatory politics of need interpretation" (1990: 118); she defines justice as based on the mutual recognition and affirmation of group differences (1990: 170–91). Anna Yeatman argues for a "participatory democratic construction of a politics of voice and representation" which provides a criterion of which differences are acceptable, which unacceptable (1993: 231).[9] But there is a problem with all these arguments for common themes that can unify the politics of difference: any advocacy of unity must, by definition, elide some differences. But eliding differences is anathema to the politics of difference. If differences are constitutive, they cannot be set aside arbitrarily. Yet the politics of difference provides no obvious way of justifying the eliding of some differences, the emphasis on others. Further, the politics of difference provides no method of argumentation by which this and other issues can be decided. Jettisoning the modernist metanarrative of logic, the politics of difference offers no viable replacement.

Questions arising out of the politics of difference are closely connected to another issue that is perhaps the most contentious in contemporary feminism: postmodernism. The question of difference is, for many feminists, inseparable from that of postmodernism. The issue of the relationship between feminism and postmodernism is complex (Hekman 1990); the outcome of this debate will effect all aspects of feminist theory. At the heart of the debate is epistemology. The root question is whether the anti-foundational stance of postmodernism is compatible with feminism and, most specifically, a feminist politics. Postmodernism defines a world without metanarratives, without absolutes. Advocates of a postmodern feminism argue that we should adopt this definition and accept the challenge of creating a feminist politics that does not seek Truth.[10] But these arguments are not persuasive to feminists who want a stable ground for feminist theory and practice. Most feminists today are convinced that we must do more than accommodate difference in feminism: we must bring it to the center of feminist theory and politics. But most also remain convinced that postmodernism is not the appropriate avenue for this accommodation. Thus some theorists have tried to fashion a kind of epistemological middle ground between what I have called the second strategy and postmodernism.[11]

That such a compromise is inadequate for answering the epistemological questions posed by postmodernism is revealed in the most comprehensive attempt to accomplish this goal, Teresa Ebert's *Ludic Feminism and After* (1996). Ebert's thesis is that it is only through critical, dialectical knowledge that feminism can seriously engage the existing social arrangements and change them. What she calls "ludic postmodernism" has, she claims, reached an epistemological impasse with its emphasis on the discursive constructedness of practice. Against this, Ebert advocates "historical materialist critique" – knowledge practice that historically situates the possibilities of what exists under patriarchal capitalist relations of difference and points to what is suppressed by the empirically existing (1996: 6–7). This approach, which, Ebert claims, possesses the potential for producing transformative knowledge, is "resistance postmodernism" (1996: 16).

Central to Ebert's critique is her discussion of the role of "experience" in feminist thought. Her thesis is that the resistance to theory in what she calls ludic postmodernism has resulted in an understanding of experience as exclusively local and, most significantly, self-explanatory. Against this, Ebert argues that experience, like all cultural and political practices, is interrelated with other practices and can only be explained from its outside. Theory, she claims, explains this outside – it demonstrates that the difference of experience is global, historical, and already determined by the material forces of production (1996: 19). The theory that Ebert advocates – what she calls "a new red feminism" – would replace ludic feminism's local, piecemeal knowledge with knowledge of "social totality." Her contention is that it is only through such knowledge that radical social change is possible. Reading the social as the site of infinite differences, she claims, is an ideological alibi for rendering revolution an impossibility (1996: 85–7).

The question of difference and its role in feminist theory is central to Ebert's analysis. She notes the change in the concept of difference from what I have called the first and second strategies. What she objects to in ludic postmodernism is also related to difference: she claims that ludic postmodernism proliferates differences without distinctions, that it, in a sense, wallows in and is swallowed by difference. Against this, Ebert argues that some differences matter more than others; differences must be understood in relation to a system of exploitation. Specifically, she argues that the material reality of labor provides an objective reality by which differences can be measured. Resistance postmodernism, she claims, situates differences between women in the social totality. It holds onto the "objective reality" of the material conditions of women's lives while engaging the interaction of various other elements. She concludes that differences within class societies are always exploitative. Thus the goal of a transformative feminism must be to end differences, not exploit them (1996: 134–71).

The virtue of Ebert's analysis is that she, more so than many of the critics of postmodern feminism, has diagnosed the problem posed by an overemphasis on difference in feminist theory. First, she understands that focusing on the multitude of different experiences of women is self-defeating for feminist theory. She also understands that experience is not self-explanatory, a "given" that requires no interpretation. Understanding experience, like understanding any social phenomenon, requires abstraction and conceptualization. Further, merely cataloging the proliferation of different experiences that women engage in does little to foster an understanding of gender exploitation. Her second point with regard to difference is equally significant: some differences are more important than others. Ebert grounds this statement in the assertion of an objective, material reality produced by labor. Her contention is that this objective reality provides the yardstick by which the importance of differences can be measured.

Although Ebert's diagnosis of the problems that the emphasis on differences poses for feminist theory is convincing, her solution is not. Her principal thesis – that some differences are more important than others – is significant. But Ebert abandons the insightfulness of her analysis when she attempts to solve this problem. She argues that some of the differences that society has constructed around gender are trivial, while others define the parameters of women's lives. From this she concludes that the only way we can differentiate among these differences is to posit an objective material reality and a social totality that can be apprehended. This conclusion does not necessarily follow from Ebert's analysis. There is no reason to suppose that the only solution to the problem of difference is the construction, or reconstruction, of a grounding metanarrative. There are many reasons to suppose the opposite, however. Feminists tried this in the second strategy, positing "women's experience" as the grounding truth of social reality. Ebert herself argues that this strategy did not work. She should see that appealing to another absolute, objective material reality, will not work either. Ebert is right that we need a new epistemology/methodology in order to accommodate difference. But she is looking for it in the wrong place.

The future of differences

There is a growing consensus in feminist theory that we are witnessing a paradigm shift in the 1990s.[12] We are rejecting modernist epistemology in all its guises: the Cartesian subject, de-gendered, autonomous, rational; the search for an aperspectival objectivity and universality; the neat binarisms stemming from the dichotomy of the masculine/feminine. This paradigm shift is not, of course, limited to feminist theory. Late twentieth-century thought in general and epistemology in particular have been characterized by the movement from the universal to the particular, from Truth to truths. Like any paradigm shift, this movement solves some problems and raises others. In epistemology it solves or, rather, displaces the question of how universal truth is grounded, but it raises the equally difficult question of how to justify particular truths.[13]

In the context of this paradigm shift the problems encountered by feminist epistemologists are both typical of this movement and unique because of the peculiar position of feminism relative to the knowledge establishment. Feminists have a particularly urgent reason for wanting to provide a justification for the truth claims that they advance. Feminism is positioned outside the discourse of truth and knowledge that constitutes the modernist paradigm. Feminists claim not just that this discourse does not presently include women, but that it cannot be reformulated to do so. The feminist claim that women are and have been oppressed, therefore, must be grounded in a wholly different definition of truth and knowledge. The feminist assault on the bastions of knowledge was easier to justify when feminists pursued the first and second strategies discussed above: both these strategies presupposed that the universal truth of modernist epistemology had to be altered, but this truth nevertheless remained intact as a goal of theory. The paradigm of differences problematizes this goal. In the terms of this paradigm, truth is plural and relative, historical and particular. This truth requires a new understanding of how claims are grounded, and, specifically, a new means of arguing for the truth of feminist claims over rival claims to truth.

Feminist claims to truth exhibit another peculiarity: unlike other epistemological assaults on modernism, they are tied to a political movement. Speaking for "women" has been the centerpiece of both the first and second strategies of mid-twentieth-century feminism. The third strategy, if, indeed, we can yet call it that, is, in contrast, centered around the deconstruction of the concept of "woman." The epistemological and practical/political problems caused by this are wide-ranging. In feminist discussions today, speaking for "woman" is necessarily suspect. Many, if not most, feminists have embraced Elizabeth Spelman's thesis that the concept "woman" is necessarily essentializing and hierarchical (1988).[14] Yet the consequences of this thesis are only beginning to be felt. Many feminists are asking how we can have a feminist politics without "woman." The foregoing discussion of the difficulty of defining a feminist politics of difference is a case in point.

In 1996 *Signs* published a collective interview of feminist theorists and practitioners that centered around these issues (Hartmann et al. 1996). One of the themes that emerged from this discussion of what might be called an epistemology and practice of differences is pragmatism: not "Pragmatism" in the sense of the American philosophical movement of the early twentieth century, but pragmatism in the sense of an attempt to justify a methodology and a politics by the criterion of usefulness. In the absence of a universal metanarrative that can adjudicate questions of truth, pragmatism, usefulness, has come to the fore in many feminist discussions.[15]

In her insightful analyses of the problems confronting feminist epistemology, Lorraine Code argues that what we need is a "new geography of the epistemic terrain" (1995: 52). She asserts that we are undergoing a paradigm shift that calls for the replacement of methodological monism by methodological pluralism. The paradigm shift that we are currently witnessing, she argues, is unlikely to produce a single, universal criterion of assessment (1995: 161). To deal with this situation, she concludes, feminists should "come out" as relativists, not in order to argue for relativism as opposed to absolutism, but to refuse the dichotomies of traditional epistemology (1995: 186). We need to "wipe the universalist slate clean" and work with the creative opportunities that this provides (1995: 194).

The goal of this book is to continue the task of mapping the new epistemic terrain into which feminism is moving. That this mapping has already begun is obvious; the epistemology of differences is everywhere in feminist theory and practice. But, as with any paradigm shift, much mopping up needs to be done after a revolutionary shift. This book is Kuhnian in spirit: I assume that the paradigm shift has taken place and that it is now necessary for us to clarify the parameters of the new paradigm.

I should be clear at the outset that I do not define this paradigm shift as synonymous with a move from modernist to postmodernist thought. Appealing to postmodernism will not meet the challenge facing feminism, for a number of important reasons. First, postmodernism is, as Ebert so graphically illustrates, a diverse phenomenon. Claiming that feminism should ally itself with postmodernism thus raises more questions than it answers: Precisely which postmodernism should be the basis of the alliance? Can we reject Derrida and accept Foucault, or must we embrace both? Second, and most importantly, many postmodern thinkers refuse to define postmodernism as constituting a new paradigm. They argue instead that postmodernism is beyond paradigms, that it does not dictate a new epistemology but, rather, rejects the whole notion of epistemology. I think this position is both wrongheaded and self-defeating. Unless we acknowledge that we have indeed entered a new epistemological space, we cannot get on with the important task of defining that space. Embracing the postmodernist views of many contemporary theorists leaves us without guidance on many key methodological and epistemological issues facing feminist thought.

In the following I approach the task of defining a new paradigm for what I am calling the third strategy by breaking it down into two components: methodology and epistemology. I argue that feminists must develop a means of justifying the concepts we employ in the truth claims we advance. Specifically, we must develop a methodology that justifies general concepts such as "woman" and "gender" that elide differences among women, as well as the more particular concepts called for by the emphasis on differences. In order to accomplish this goal, I turn to the work of Max Weber. I argue that his methodological approach and, specifically, his concept of the ideal type provide an understanding of and justification for the concepts that feminists use. Most significantly, they also provide a justification for the general concepts necessary to feminist social-scientific analysis and critique. Although there have been extensive feminist critiques of the concepts of the natural sciences, little comparable work has been done in the social sciences. I attempt to rectify this through a detailed analysis of concept formation in feminist social science.

The second component of my argument is the effort to develop an epistemology of truths rather than Truth. I argue that feminism must provide a grounding for truth claims that does not rely on a universal metanarrative but nevertheless provides a stable basis for meaning. I develop an epistemology of multiple truths by examining, first, moral discourse and, second, the discourse of epistemology. In both of these examinations my motive is pragmatic: I attempt to define strategies by which feminists can displace the hegemony of the discourse of Truth and replace it with a discourse of truths. My guiding principle in these discussions is that feminists must avoid two pitfalls: the retreat to a new form of universalism and the surrender to an "anything goes" relativism. My goal is to develop an epistemological and methodological groundwork for a feminism of differences that continues the tradition of social critique that has been and continues to be the hallmark of feminist theory.

2

From Difference to Differences: The Case of Feminist Standpoint Theory

In the first chapter I sketched in broad terms the thesis of this book: that a paradigm shift is occurring in feminist thought, from an emphasis on difference to the exploration of differences. Central to this thesis was the claim that this new paradigm represents a radical repudiation of the dichotomous epistemology that dominates modernist thought. My conclusion to this argument was that this new paradigm requires a new epistemology and methodology that is only beginning to emerge in feminist thought.[1]

In the course of articulating this thesis, I advanced two corollary theses. The first was that the two strategies outlined by de Beauvoir – first, the erasure of difference, and, second, the emphasis on and valorization of difference – were doomed before they were even attempted. Because both strategies are rooted in the modernist epistemology of gendered dichotomies, no amount of tinkering with that epistemology will result in the achievement of de Beauvoir's goal of "women's liberation." The second corollary was the claim that, as feminists shifted from the first to the second strategy, indications of the deconstruction of the gendered dichotomies that informed the two strategies began to emerge. The central indication of this deconstruction was the shift from an emphasis on biology to an emphasis on social construction. This shift had a profound effect on feminist theory and practice. It highlighted the contingency of the masculine/ feminine hierarchy and, hence, its malleability. It also focused feminist attention on the diversity of social forces that construct the feminine. What became obvious from these explorations was that although certain overarching similarities in the constitution of the feminine can be identified, the differences among women are at least as significant. Race, class, sexual orientation, age, and a host of other factors impinge on the construction of the feminine in fundamental ways. Feminists began to argue that these factors are constitutive of the identity of individual women; they cannot be dismissed as incidental to the general category of "woman." This growing realization called for a fundamental change in the second strategy. A difficult question came to the forefront of feminist thought: how can the goal of feminist theory be the emphasis on, and valorization of, "woman's difference" if "woman" is a diverse and multifaceted category?

This chapter focuses on these two corollary theses. Several considerations dictate this tactic. An analysis of these theses establishes a continuity in feminist thought in the twentieth century. Although my principal claim is that feminism represents, and is at the forefront of, the paradigm shift that is currently under way, this thesis is strengthened rather than weakened by the claim that this paradigm shift was foreshadowed by the work of de Beauvoir, if not earlier. The point of my discussion of de Beauvoir was to establish that the inferiority of women is a necessary consequence of the modernist epistemology she employs. It follows from this that the rejection of that epistemology was, in a sense, inevitable from the outset.

Further, arguing for these corollary theses demonstrates that contemporary feminism can draw on and identify with the history of feminist thought in the twentieth century. There is a disturbing tendency among some contemporary feminists, especially those who identify themselves as postmoderns, to reject earlier feminist thought – what I call the first and second strategies – as naive and deluded, certainly not worthy of serious attention today. I hope to demonstrate in the following analysis that we have much to learn from previous feminist thought, precisely because it is the groundwork on which contemporary feminism rests. Although today we may proclaim a paradigm shift and declare that this shift was inevitable, this does not entail that all previous feminist thought is worthless because it was epistemologically misguided.

I focus here on a particularly prominent example of the second strategy's emphasis on difference: feminist standpoint theory. Feminist standpoint theory is exemplary in a number of ways. First, this approach, and particularly the version articulated by Nancy Hartsock in *Money, Sex, and Power* (1983c), was one of the most influential forces in feminist theory in the 1980s. Its Marxist roots provided a bridge between Marxism and feminism that many feminists embraced. Most importantly, it provided an articulation of the second strategy that was intellectually and politically respectable. Because of its Marxist roots, feminist standpoint theory defined the valorization of women's difference as a mode of resistance rather than, as some of the critics of the second strategy claimed, a mode of accommodation. Second, feminist standpoint theory, and particularly the work of Hartsock, has been centrally interested in questions of epistemology and method as they relate to feminist theory and politics. Hartsock proclaimed the goal of her theory as defining the nature of the truth claims that feminists advance and providing a methodological grounding that validates those claims. For Hartsock, questions of method and epistemology are inseparable from questions of power and politics.

Third, the evolution of feminist standpoint theory in the 1980s and early 1990s provides one of the best illustrations of the way in which feminist theorists struggled with the emerging issue of differences among women. In light of this interest, feminist standpoint theorists – and, again, Hartsock's work stands out as exemplary – did not continue to argue dogmatically for *the* standpoint of women. Rather, as feminists began to explore the diversity of social constructions that impinge on variously situated women, feminist standpoint theorists tried to accommodate these insights. Specifically, they attempted to theorize about multiple standpoints without abandoning one of the cornerstones of feminist standpoint theory: the claim that there is a truth to social reality that can be known in its totality.

Fourth, feminist standpoint theory also illustrates the phenomenon mentioned above: the tendency of contemporary feminists to dismiss earlier feminist theories. Today, feminist standpoint theory is frequently regarded as a quaint relic of feminism's less sophisticated past. Several developments have led to this declining influence. The inspiration for feminist standpoint theory, Marxism, has been discredited in both theory and practice. Just as significantly, feminist standpoint theory appears to be at odds with the issue that has dominated feminist debate in the 1990s: difference. The approach appears to presume a single feminist standpoint rather than, as the emphasis on differences demands, multiple standpoints. Finally, feminist standpoint theory appears to be opposed to one of the most significant influences in recent feminist theory: postmodernism/poststructuralism. The Marxist roots of the theory seem to contradict what many define as the anti-materialism of postmodernism. For all these reasons, many contemporary feminists have concluded that feminist standpoint theory should be discarded.[2]

This conclusion is premature; it is a mistake to write off feminist standpoint theory too quickly. Feminist standpoint theory makes a bold attempt to define the nature of women's oppression and root its claims in an understanding of the nature of social reality. Hartsock's definition of feminist standpoint theory was initially formulated in the context of Marxist politics. Following the lead of Marxism, feminist standpoint theorists recognized that feminist politics demands a justification for the truth claims of feminist theory and that this justification lies in an understanding of the true nature of social reality. Thus, from the outset, epistemology and politics, truth and power, were linked. Throughout its development, feminist standpoint theorists' quest for truth and politics has been shaped by two central understandings: that knowledge is situated and perspectival, and that there are multiple standpoints from which knowledge is produced. As the theory developed, feminist standpoint theorists explored, first, how knowledge can be situated yet "true," and, second, how we can acknowledge difference without obviating the possibility of critique and thus a viable feminist politics. Feminist standpoint theorists have answered these questions in a variety of ways; many of these answers have been unsatisfactory; the theory has been frequently reformulated. In the course of working out their arguments, however, these theorists were instrumental in changing the direction of feminist theory.

Defining the feminist standpoint

Two versions of feminist standpoint theory emerged in the 1970s and 1980s: a philosophical version articulated by Nancy Hartsock and a sociological version articulated primarily by Dorothy Smith. Hartsock's version is more useful for my purposes, because she focuses on the epistemological and methodological issues that I am investigating. In an article first published in *Quest* in 1975, Hartsock wrote: "At bottom feminism is a mode of analysis, a method of approaching life and politics, rather than a set of political conclusions about the oppression of women" (1981: 35). The power of feminist method, she asserts, grows out of the fact that it enables us to connect every-day life with the analysis of the social institutions that shape that life (1981: 36). This early article reveals the presupposition that defines her later formulation of the feminist standpoint: the belief that feminism, while necessarily political, at the same time must be centrally concerned with method, truth, and epistemology. But this early article also raises an issue that will complicate Hartsock's search for truth in a feminist mode. She notes that the reality perceived by different segments of society is varied. Thus, she concludes, "Feminism as a mode of analysis leads us to respect experience and differences, to respect people enough to believe that they are in the best possible position to make their own revolution" (1981: 40).

For Hartsock, activity is epistemology: women and men create their own realities through their different activities and experiences. If this were the whole story, however, then both truth and reality would be multiple, even "relative," and Hartsock is very concerned to avoid this conclusion. When she presents her theory of the feminist standpoint in *Money, Sex, and Power* (1983c), this is the focus of her attention. She insists that "the concept of a standpoint rests on the fact that there are some perspectives on society from which, however well intentioned one may be, the real relations of humans with each other and with the natural world are not visible" (1983c: 117). Hartsock's goal in the book is to define the concept of a standpoint and apply it to the case of women.

Hartsock outlines five criteria of a standpoint that she adapts from Marx's theory (1983c: 118). Two potentially contradictory definitions of reality structure this discussion. First, in what today would be called a social constructionist argument, Hartsock asserts that material life structures and sets limits to an understanding of social relations. It follows that reality will be perceived differently as material situations differ. It also follows that the dominant (ruling) group in society will label its perspective as "real" and reject other definitions. Second, Hartsock insists that while the ruling group's perception of reality is "partial and perverse," that of the oppressed is not – that it exposes "real" relations among humans and is hence liberatory. Throughout her work Hartsock struggles with the relationship between these two definitions of reality. It constitutes a kind of fault line that runs through her articulation of the feminist standpoint. Although her formulation has changed over the years, she continues to maintain *both* that reality is socially and materially constructed *and* that some perceptions of reality are partial, others true and liberatory.

Further aspects of feminist standpoint theory emerge in Hartsock's well-known article "The feminist standpoint" (1983b). In this article Hartsock states that a specifically feminist historical materialism "might enable us to lay bare the laws of tendency which constitute the structure of patriarchy over time" (1983b: 283). Her dualistic concept of reality structures this discussion as well. On one hand, social constructionist themes recur throughout the argument: "I will sketch out a kind of ideal type of the social relations and world view characteristic of male and female activity in order to explore the epistemology contained in the institutionalized sexual division of labor" (1983b: 289). The feminist standpoint "expresses female experience at a particular time and place, located within a particular set of social relations" (1983b: 303). Quickly following this, however, is the statement that the feminist standpoint allows us to "go beneath the surface of appearances to reveal the real but concealed social relations" (1983b: 304). Her thesis is that "women's lives make available a particular and privileged vantage point on male supremacy" (1983b: 284).

In this article Hartsock introduces an approach that will become closely identified with standpoint theory and the second strategy in general: object-relations theory. The introduction of this theory highlights the tension inherent in her concept of reality – in a sense widening the fault line in that concept. In her discussion Hartsock appeals to object-relations theory to explain the difference between the male and female experiences of the world (1983b: 296). Bringing object-relations theory to bear on her Marxist assumptions, Hartsock argues that if material life structures consciousness, then women's relationally defined existence structures a life in which dichotomies are foreign and what she calls "abstract masculinity" is exposed as partial and perverse (1983b: 298–9). Implicit in Hartsock's discussion is the assumption that object-relations theory is an appropriate and useful addition to feminist standpoint theory, not a major departure. In the context of her theory it seems to fit nicely with the Marxist thesis that reality is socially constructed and supplies a needed gendered component to that theory.

The incorporation of object-relations theory, however, represents a major theoretical departure in the development of standpoint theory. Feminist standpoint theory's identification with object-relations theory has changed the focus of the approach in three respects. First, object-relations theory, unlike Marxist theory, lacks a distinction between socially constructed and "true" reality. As feminist theorists in the 1980s discovered, object-relations theory effectively jettisons the concept of objective reality. Some advocates of feminist standpoint theory see this as an advantage, others as a disadvantage. But it becomes a problem that must be continually negotiated. Second, the incorporation of object-relations theory further problematizes the issue of difference. What was merely a troubling issue in feminist standpoint theory is a major stumbling block in object-relations theory. In object-relations theory the opposition between *the* experience of men and *the* experience of women is the centerpiece of the theory. The difficulty of theorizing differences among women and the variety of women's experiences that characterizes object-relations theory now becomes a major problem in feminist standpoint theory as well.[3] Third, the incorporation of object-relations theory into Marxist-inspired feminist standpoint theory creates an internal contradiction in the theory. For Hartsock the point of defining the difference of women from men is to promote resistance; it is a form of political opposition. Object-relations theory, by contrast, defines women's difference in traditional, pacific, even conservative terms: women are peaceful, caring, relational, and nurturing, as opposed to men, who are aggressive and autonomous. The incompatibility of these two definitions will become a significant problem for feminist standpoint theory and the second strategy in general.

In their discussion of the evolution of poststructuralist and postmodern thought, Rosalind Coward and John Ellis (1977) argue that the groundwork for the discursive concept of the subject that has become the new paradigm of subjectivity is already present in Marx's historically constituted subject. Hartsock's early definitions of feminist standpoint theory support a parallel thesis regarding the relationship between feminist standpoint theory and what I am calling the new paradigm of knowledge. The clearest way to illustrate this is to interpret Hartsock's criteria for a standpoint from the perspective of the work of a theorist who, on my definition, although not on his, represents the new paradigm – Michel Foucault. Hartsock argues, first, that material life structures and sets limits to the understanding of social relations; second, that the ruling class structures the material relations of a society and hence its definition of the "real"; and, third, that the vision available to oppressed groups must be achieved through struggle. All of this translates nicely into Foucault's theory. First, his theories of sexuality, bio-power, the carceral society, and the evolution of the Western subject provide detailed analyses of how material/social life structures consciousness. Second, one of Foucault's central aims is to define how and to what extent hegemonic discourses (what Hartsock calls the ideology of the ruling class) define "reality" in any given society. Third, he is centrally concerned with defining how subjugated knowledges (the vision of the oppressed) can be articulated (1980: 82).

But here the similarity ends. Hartsock further claims that the ruling group's vision is partial and perverse, and that the vision of the oppressed exposes the "real" relations among humans. Foucault would counter that all visions are "partial and perverse," in the sense that all knowledge is necessarily from some perspective; we must speak from somewhere, and that somewhere is constitutive of our knowledge. Most important, he would insist that the vision of the oppressed is itself another discourse, not the apprehension of "true" reality. It is undoubtedly a counter-discourse, a discourse that seeks to break the hold of the hegemonic discourse, but it is no closer to "reality" than the discourse it exposes. The most he would claim is that it may be closer to a definition of a less repressive society.

It is my contention that the deconstruction of the concept of "true" reality is already implicit in Hartsock's definition of the feminist standpoint, just as the deconstruction of the transcendent subject was implicit in Marx's theory of the social construction of consciousness. If material life structures consciousness, if the different experiences of different groups create different realities, then this must hold for the oppressed as well as the oppressor. Hartsock might reply that the oppressed's conception of reality is true because it is based on a correct perception of material reality, while that of the oppressor is false because it does not. But such an argument begs the question of how a correct perception of material reality is achieved. Ultimately, it must presuppose this reality as a given, as the standard by which truth and falsity are defined. Even in her early formulations of feminist standpoint theory, Hartsock is defensive about the accuracy of the oppressed/women's conception of reality. The incorporation of object-relations theory makes her defense of this position even more difficult. If, as object-relations theory claims, our relations with others define our perceptions, then selecting one of these perceptions as "real" is instantly suspect. But Hartsock also realizes the centrality of this point. Unless women's standpoint can be shown to be truer, a reflection of reality itself, why bother with feminist analysis at all?

One of Hartsock's major claims is that while the discourse of the ruling class is ideological, that of the oppressed is not: it reflects the concrete reality of their lives. An important aspect of this claim is her assertion that the feminist standpoint is achieved, not given. The nature of their oppression is not obvious to all women; it is only through feminist analysis that the feminist standpoint can be articulated. What this comes down to is that although the feminist standpoint is discursively constituted, the material reality of women's lives on which it is based is not. This important distinction is lost, however, in the sociological version of feminist standpoint theory. The belief that the standpoint(s) of women resists the discursive constitution that defines all "partial and perverse" perceptions of reality becomes a major theme of the sociological version of feminist standpoint theory, structuring its effort to define a distinctive method for feminist analysis.

The clearest example of this belief is the work of Dorothy Smith. In her influential article, "Women's perspective as a radical critique of sociology" (1987b),[4] Smith posits a contrast between the categories of sociology and the everyday life (what phenomenologists call the lifeworld) of women. She argues that the categories of sociology and sociological method embody what Hartsock calls "abstract masculinity." For the sociologist, objectivity is defined as the separation between knower and known, removal from the situatedness of knowledge. This method and these categories, she argues, obviate the experience of women, an experience that is always situated, relational, and engaged. Two conclusions follow from this. First, the lived reality of women's lives is absent from the domain of sociology; it is quite literally invisible to the sociologist. Without concepts to grasp that reality, sociology cannot "know" anything about it. Second, the woman sociologist experiences a bifurcated consciousness: the abstract, conceptual world she encounters as a sociologist versus her lived reality as a woman (1987b: 90). The goal of Smith's work is to define a "reorganized sociology" that would solve both these problems by foregrounding actual lived experiences.

Smith outlines this reorganized sociology, what she calls a sociology for women, in *The Everyday World as Problematic* (1987a).[5] She defines the world of sociology as a *conceptual* world divorced from the lived, actual world of everyday experience. The world of women, by contrast, is "material and local," the world as we actually experience it. These definitions lead Smith to her articulation of "women's standpoint" as the point outside textually mediated discourses in the actuality of everyday lives (1987a: 107). The standpoint of women, she claims, is related to Marx's method but constitutes an improvement on it because it is "anchored" in the everyday world (1987a: 142). This method constitutes the "Copernican shift in sociology" that Smith is seeking (1979: 183).

Smith is quite clear about what she is attempting to do in her work; whether she is successful is another matter. She posits an absolute dichotomy between abstract concepts on one hand and lived reality on the other, indicts sociology for inhabiting the conceptual world of abstractions, and advocates a move to the other side of the dichotomy. One of the curious aspects of Smith's account is that, although it is inspired by phenomenological method, it nevertheless departs from the phenomenologist's understanding of the nature of concept formation and the role of concepts in sociological analysis. Alfred Schutz, whose theory of the lifeworld is the origin of Smith's approach, claims, like Smith, that sociological method must be rooted in the lived actuality of the social actors' reality (the lifeworld), and that the lived experiences of social actors must form the basis of sociological method and concepts (Schutz 1962, 1964, 1967). But, unlike Smith, Schutz argues, first, that the social actors' world is constituted by their concepts, and, second, that the sociologist also employs concepts in order to study that lifeworld. Schutz claims that the sociology of the lifeworld that he advocates is more "adequate" than positivist sociology because, unlike that sociology, it is rooted in the concepts of social actors. But he also makes it clear that his method is itself a complex conceptual apparatus with standards of truth and accuracy – that is, a discursive formation.

Two points are crucial to Schutz's account. First, he makes an explicit argument for a sociology based on one set of concepts – those of the social actors – rather than another set of concepts – concepts created by the social scientist that are unrelated to those of the social actors. He does not assume that this approach to sociology is, *prima facie*, superior; he argues for it against the alternatives. Second, although Schutz claims that the lifeworld of the social actors is constituted by concepts, he also claims that these concepts form the basis of, but are not identical to, the concepts of the social scientist.

At times Smith seems to acknowledge that she is, in fact, advocating a *conceptual* shift, and not a shift from concepts to reality. She asserts: "I am not suggesting, of course, that sociology can be done without knowing how to do it and that we approach our work with a naive consciousness" (1979: 174). In an explicit reference to Schutz, she claims that "as we evolve a discourse among women, it crystallizes the issues and concerns of those of us who got there first and have defined the types of statements, the relevances, the phenomenal universe, and the conventions that give it a social form independent of the particular individuals who are active in it" (1987a: 221). But these are isolated references. The overall thrust of her work is to deny that she is either studying a *conceptual* reality (the world of the social actors) or fashioning a discourse and advocating a method. Her constantly reiterated thesis is that her approach is superior to "abstract sociology" because it is rooted in "an actual material setting, an actual local and particular place in the world" (1979: 181).

What she refuses to acknowledge is that this "reality" too is discursively constituted. To do so would be to abandon the neat dichotomy between abstract concepts and lived reality on which her approach rests.[6]

Other early formulations of feminist standpoint theory reflect this supposed dichotomy between concepts and reality: specifically, between the abstract world of men and the concrete world of women. Hilary Rose (1983, 1986) conceptualizes the dichotomy in terms of the material reality of women's labor and abstract masculinist science; Iris Young calls for a "feminist historical materialism" rooted in "real social relations" (1980: 184–5); Mary O'Brien (1981) looks to the reproductive process to provide the material basis for her social theory; Alison Jaggar (1983) appeals to an explicitly Marxist understanding of the epistemological advantages of the oppressed view of reality. Even Jane Flax (1983), who later repudiates any naive conception of reality, argues that we need ways of thinking that can do justice to our experience.

Despite their significant differences, all these accounts share the conviction that the feminist standpoint is rooted in a "reality" that is the opposite of the abstract conceptual world inhabited by men, particularly men of the ruling class, and that in this reality lies the truth of the human condition. This belief involves fundamental misunderstandings both of the constitution of the social world and of the means by which social scientists seek to understand that world. These misunderstandings, furthermore, have had a particularly detrimental effect on feminist theory. The misunderstanding of the constitution of the social world is rooted in an untenable dichotomy between concepts and reality. It assumes that "reality," and in particular the reality of the social/lifeworld, is a given, a preconceptual material fact. Positing a dichotomy between concepts and reality denies that the lifeworld is, like every other human activity, discursively constituted. Social actors use concepts to describe their everyday world; these concepts constitute that world. The discourse of the lifeworld is a discourse distinct from that of abstract science, but a discourse nonetheless.[7] The misunderstanding of how social scientists grasp the social world is related to this dichotomy. As both Schutz and Max Weber clearly realized, one can argue that sociological analysis *should* begin with the actors' concepts, and that any other approach will miss the object of its study – the lifeworld – but this requires a specific *argument*. Opposing concepts to reality is not an argument and, furthermore, results in a misconception of the nature of social science.

The challenge of difference: redefining the feminist standpoint

The original formulations of feminist standpoint theory rest on two assumptions: that all knowledge is located and situated, and that one location, that of the standpoint of women, is privileged because it provides a vantage point that reveals the truth of social reality. It is my thesis that the deconstruction of this second assumption is implicit in the first, and that as the theory developed, the problematic nature of the second assumption came to the forefront. More specifically, my argument is that as feminists began to explore the constitution of knowledge as situated and perspectival, the assumption of one true location for knowledge became increasingly untenable. Situated knowledge is, by definition, plural. It necessarily acknowledges the differences and diversity of the constitution of knowledge; it is incompatible with the concept of totalizing knowledge. Another way of putting this thesis is that a new paradigm of knowledge was implicit in the first formulations of feminist standpoint theory, but that these first formulations retained elements of the paradigm being replaced.

I argued in chapter 1 that the paradigm shift in feminist thought is not an isolated phenomenon but, rather, part of a general shift in late twentieth-century thought. Epistemologists have devoted much attention to the concept of "reality" in the past several decades, offering powerful arguments against the notion of a given, preconceptual reality that grounds knowledge. The "linguistic turn" of twentieth-century philosophy and the influence of hermeneutics, postmodernism, and poststructuralism have all contributed to the present skepticism about "reality." These speculations are directly relevant to the evolution of feminist standpoint theory, an approach initially grounded in just such a concept of reality. But it was another discussion, a discussion specific to the feminist community, that stimulated a reassessment of feminist standpoint theory in the late 1980s and early 1990s. Originally, feminist standpoint theorists claimed that the standpoint of women offers a privileged vantage point for knowledge. But as the theory evolved, it became obvious that if the experiences of women create knowledge and reality, then it must be the case that this knowledge and reality are plural, because the experiences of women are varied and diverse. The subsequent reevaluation of feminist standpoint theory was an attempt to reconstitute the theory from the perspective of these differences.

This reevaluation focused on two issues that are central to the future of feminist theory and politics. First, if we acknowledge, as we must, that there are many realities that women inhabit, this necessarily affects the status of the truth claims that feminists advance. One cannot appeal to one true reality to ground claims about social reality if there is more than one such reality; if there are multiple realities, then there must be multiple truths that correspond to them. Second, if we abandon a single axis of analysis, *the* standpoint of women, and instead try to accommodate the multiple, potentially infinite number of standpoints of diverse women, we are in danger of losing the analytic force of our argument. Or, in other words, if we try to accommodate an infinite number of axes of analysis, our arguments seem destined to slip into hopeless confusion.[8] These issues have more than methodological significance; furthermore, they impinge on the possibility of a feminist politics. The political corollary to both issues is the concern that if we abandon the monolithic concept of "woman" implicit in *the* feminist standpoint, the possibility of a cohesive feminist politics is jeopardized.

The concern both to accommodate difference and to preserve the analytic and political force of feminist theory, specifically feminist standpoint theory, is prominent in the subsequent work of Nancy Hartsock. It is obvious that Hartsock cares very deeply about these issues. She is painfully aware of the evils of racism, particularly within the women's movement. She is also passionately committed to feminist social criticism as a force for social change and is determined not to let forces such as postmodernism erode that potential. These concerns emerge forcefully in her 1987 article "Rethinking modernism." The point of departure for Hartsock's argument is the differences among women. She asserts that we need to develop an understanding of difference by creating a politics in which previously marginalized groups can name themselves and participate in defining the terms that structure their world (1987: 189). Central to Hartsock's argument is the claim that unless we provide a systematic understanding of the world, we will be unable to change it. The object of her polemic in this and several other articles is postmodernism. In the past decade the issues of difference and multiplicity have come to be closely identified with postmodernism. Hartsock wants to reject this identification. She wants to valorize difference, to claim that the differences among women are significant both theoretically and practically, yet at the same time reject postmodernism on the grounds that it obviates the possibility of the systemic knowledge that is necessary for social change.

Hartsock's efforts both to valorize difference and to retain at least some notion of reality and truth, of the "way the world is," produce some odd results. In "Rethinking modernism," she significantly alters the basic thesis of feminist standpoint theory by asserting that although women are not a unitary group, white, ruling class, Eurocentric men are (1987: 192). The ruling class, now referred to as the "center," is defined as unitary, while those on the periphery, the "others," are defined as heterogeneous. Hartsock's argument is that we must create a politics that lets the "others" into the center, a center which, she claims, will "obviously" look different when occupied by women and men of color (1987: 201). Hartsock's solution raises some troubling questions. It posits a center that is heterogeneous rather than homogeneous, which suggests that it may not be a "center" at all. Further, positing the movement of the "others" into the center effectively eliminates the periphery. We can, I think, assume that Hartsock would not endorse a politics in which any group was marginalized. But it is difficult to retain the concept of a "center," as she does, without a corresponding concept of periphery.[9]

All these questions could be quite easily eliminated by abandoning the center/periphery dichotomy. But Hartsock is adamantly opposed to such a move. For those of us who have been constituted as "other," she states, we must insist on a world in which we are at the center rather than on the periphery.[10] The postmoderns who want to eliminate the center, she claims, thereby deny us our right of self-definition. She also claims that they deny us the right to speak the truth about our subjugation, obviating the very possibility of knowledge and truth. Informing all of Hartsock's recent work is a fundamental dichotomy: either we have systemic knowledge of the way the world is, or we have no knowledge, no truth, and no politics. For Hartsock, postmodernism represents the second term of this dichotomy. I could (and, in the last chapter, do) argue, against Hartsock, that truth, knowledge, and politics are possible without an absolute grounding, and, further, that some postmodern writers make this argument quite persuasively. But there is a more fruitful way of approaching Hartsock's argument in this context. Postmodern thinkers, as Fraser and Nicholson have so famously argued (1990), are not necessarily concerned with politics; feminists, by contrast, necessarily are. Hartsock's fear that the proliferation of differences in feminist theory threatens the basis of feminist theory and practice is not frivolous – it is a legitimate concern. If, as Hartsock realizes we must, feminism abandons *the* feminist standpoint and, with it, *the* correct view of reality, then we are in danger of abandoning the whole point of feminist analysis and politics: revealing the oppression of "women" and arguing for a less repressive society. If there are multiple feminist standpoints, then there must be multiple truths and multiple realities. This is a difficult position for those who want to change the world according to a new image – that is, for feminists.

Hartsock has correctly defined the problem facing feminist theory but is pursuing a solution in the wrong direction. She wants to embrace the "situated knowledges" that Haraway and others have theorized, but she cannot accept the logical consequence of this position: that no perspective/standpoint is epistemologically privileged. She wants to retain a notion of privileged knowledge that can accommodate both diversity and locatedness. But her attempts to achieve this goal are not successful. "Situated knowledges," she claims, are "located in a particular time and place. They are therefore partial. They do not see everything from nowhere but they do see some things from somewhere." Borrowing postmodern terminology, she refers to the knowledges produced from the various subject positions of different women as "the epistemologies of these marked subjectivities." She then goes on to argue: "The struggles they represent and express, if made self-conscious, can go beyond efforts at survival to recognize the centrality of systemic power relations" (1989–90: 28–30). What this formulation requires is a sustained argument for how such systemic knowledge is possible. But Hartsock does not provide such an argument. Other feminist standpoint theorists have also attempted to deal with the challenge of difference and its implications for the truth claims of the feminist standpoint. Dorothy Smith (1990a; 1990b) gets around the problem of difference by definitional fiat: she defines "women's actually lived experience" as a category that encompasses the diversity of women's lives and activities. She then opposes this category to the abstract concepts of sociological analysis, contrasting the "ideological" categories of the sociologist to "what actually happened" – the "primary narrative" (1990a: 157). But the method that she derives from this dichotomy is flawed and incomplete. Despite the obvious influence of Schutz's work on her formulation, Smith does not offer an argument that parallels Schutz's argument for grounding social analysis in the social actors' concepts. Instead of giving reasons for why the located knowledge of women is superior to the abstract knowledge of the sociologist, Smith merely assumes this to be obvious. Further, despite frequent references to Foucault and his theory of discourse, Smith refuses to identify the women's standpoint as a knowledge-producing discursive formation. She offers a detailed discussion of how the sociologist's discursive formations constitute the instruments of state power. At times she comes close to admitting that the discourse that women have developed about their lived reality – a discourse that includes concepts such as rape, sexual harassment, and battery – is also constituted. But ultimately she shies away from this conclusion. Like Hartsock, she continues to privilege the standpoint of women, because she assumes that without such privileging the knowledge women claim loses its necessary grounding.

Patricia Hill Collins has a particular stake in theorizing difference: she wants to account for the unique standpoint of black women. She defines her problem in the context of the issue of difference: her goal, she states, is to articulate the unique aspects of black women's standpoint without denying the differences among black women. She tackles this problem by claiming that the black feminist standpoint she articulates, although rooted in everyday experiences, is constructed by the theorists who reflect on that experience. One of the goals of her own theory is to define the common experiences of black women that constitute their unique standpoint (1989; 1990: 208ff). Collins deals with the difficult issue of the truth status of the black feminist standpoint in an ambiguous way. In an early article she claims "objectivity" for the "outsider within" status of black women (1986: 15). In her more recent work, however, She retreats from this claim. In *Black Feminist Thought* she appeals to Donna Haraway's concept of standpoint as the most valid and concludes that "a Black women's standpoint is only one angle of vision," a "partial perspective" (1990: 234). But despite her endorsement of Haraway's position, Collins is unwilling to embrace the full implications of situated knowledge. She rejects the claim that the perspective of the oppressed yields "absolute truth," but she also rejects "relativism," which she defines as the claim that all visions are equal (1990: 235). Her final position holds out some hope for a redefined concept of objectivity. She asserts that black feminists who develop knowledge claims that can accommodate both black feminist epistemology and white masculinist epistemology "may have found a route to the elusive goal of generating so-called objective generalizations that can stand as universal truth." The ideas that are validated by different standpoints, she concludes, produce "the most objective truths" (1989: 773).

Other than Haraway herself, the only prominent feminist standpoint theorist to fully embrace what Collins labels the "relativist" position is Sara Ruddick. Given the anomalous position of Ruddick's thought in the difference debate, this should come as no surprise. Ruddick applies her belief that feminism challenges the universality imperative of masculine thinking to her definition of the feminist standpoint (1989: 128). In her discussion of "Maternal thinking as a feminist standpoint" Ruddick appeals to both Hartsock and Foucault, apparently seeing no contradiction between Hartsock's definition of the feminist standpoint and Foucault's theory of subjugated knowledges (1989: 130). She concludes:

> Although I count myself among standpoint theorists, I do not take the final step that some appear to take of claiming for one standpoint a truth that is exhaustive and absolute.... Although I envision a world organized by the values of caring labor, I cannot identify the grounds, reason, or god that would legitimate that vision. (1989: 135)[11]

Ruddick's solution to the problem of difference and privilege sets her apart from other feminist standpoint theorists. Like Collins and Hartsock, most advocates of the feminist standpoint are not content to define it as simply a "different voice" (or voices), one perspective among many. The most sustained attempt to deal with the epistemological questions raised by redefining feminist standpoint theory in light of the difference debate is that of Sandra Harding. In her influential *The Science Question in Feminism* (1986) Harding defines three feminist epistemologies: feminist empiricism, feminist standpoint theory, and feminist postmodernism. Although sympathetic to standpoint epistemologies, Harding is persuaded that there cannot be *one* feminist standpoint; the situations of women are too diverse. Yet she also sees problems with the postmodern alternative. On her reading, postmodernism posits fractured identities, an apolitical approach, and the rejection of any kind of knowledge that results in an absolute relativism. In this book Harding avoids choosing one epistemology over another by arguing for the necessary instability of feminist theories. Coherent theories in an incoherent world, she concludes, are either silly, uninteresting, or oppressive (1986: 164).

In *Whose Science? Whose Knowledge?* (1991) Harding appears to reverse her position by fashioning a coherent theory for feminist science. The theory she offers, however, is a blend of diverse elements and thus continues the eclectic spirit of her earlier book. The aim of the book, she states, is not to resolve all tensions and contradictions between feminism and Western science, but to "advance more useful ways for us to think about and plan their future encounters" (1991: xi). Harding defines her position as "a postmodernist standpoint approach that is nevertheless committed to rethinking and revising some important notions from conventional metatheories of science" (1991: 49). In the course of developing her approach, Harding offers both a critique and a redefinition of standpoint theory, developing "the logic of the standpoint theory in ways that more vigorously pull it away from its modernist origins and more clearly enable it to advance some postmodernist goals" (1991: 106). For Harding, standpoint theory is attractive because it offers an alternative to a crucial and seemingly irresolvable dichotomy facing feminist theory: essentialism versus relativism. Her rejection of *one* feminist standpoint avoids the danger of essentialism; relativism is defeated by her claim that we must insist on an objective location – women's lives – for the place where research should begin (1991: 134–42). But as her theory unfolds, it becomes clear that Harding does not so much deconstruct this dichotomy as locate her position along the continuum it creates.

The ubiquitous issue of relativism leads Harding to the formulation of the most distinctive element of her standpoint theory: "strong objectivity." She begins by noting that "although diversity, pluralism, relativism, and difference have their valuable and political uses, embracing them resolves the political-scientific-epistemological conflict to almost no one's satisfaction" (1991: 140). Standpoint epistemologists, she argues, embrace historical-cultural-sociological relativism while rejecting judgmental or epistemological relativism (1991: 142). The "strong objectivity" she advocates recognizes the social situatedness of all knowledge but also requires "a critical evaluation to determine which social situations tend to generate the most objective knowledge claims" (1991: 142). Harding follows traditional standpoint epistemology in assuming that it is the existence of oppression that provides the possibility of objectivity. She develops an interesting corollary of this theory, however, by arguing that higher levels of oppression provide more objective accounts: "It should be clear that if it is beneficial to start research, scholarship and theory in white women's situations, then we should be able to learn even more about the social and natural orders if we start from the situations of women in devalued and oppressed races, classes and cultures" (1991: 179–80).

Harding argues for keeping the concept of objectivity, despite its historical associations with masculinist science, because of its "glorious intellectual history" (1991: 160). The concept of objectivity she advocates departs from the masculinist definition in that it does not lay claim to "true beliefs" or "transhistorical privilege." But it also retains one important aspect of that definition: "Starting research in women's lives leads to socially constructed claims that are less false – less partial and distorted – than are the (also socially constructed) claims that result if one starts from the lives of men in the dominant groups" (1991: 185). The "less false stories" Harding advocates mediate between transhistorical universals on the one hand and absolute relativism on the other, forming a kind of middle ground between the polarities of this dichotomy. Harding intends this middle ground to be a critique of postmodern and poststructuralist positions. The postmodernists, Harding declares, assume that giving up on the goal of telling one true story about reality entails giving up on telling less false stories (1991: 187), a position that is unlikely to satisfy feminists' desire to know "how the world is" (1991: 304).

It would not be difficult to argue that Harding, like Hartsock, misinterprets the postmodern definition of knowledge, and that at least one "postmodern" writer, Foucault, is very interested in telling stories that will result in a less oppressive social order. But, again, there is a more useful way to approach Harding's argument in this context. Harding's reassessment of standpoint theory contains two serious oversights. First, she argues that starting research from the reality of women's lives, preferably those of women who are also oppressed by race and class, will lead to a more objective account of social reality. Like Hartsock, Harding offers no argument as to why this is the case. It is not enough simply to assume that Marx got it right on such a crucial point. Like Smith, Harding does not explicitly acknowledge that "the reality of women's lives" is itself a socially constructed discursive formation. It is a discourse that has been constructed, at least in part, by feminist standpoint theorists, who define it as the ground of their method. The fact that it is closely tied to the social actors' own concepts and provides a counter to the hegemonic discourse of masculinist science makes it no less a discourse. Feminist standpoint theory can and should be defined as a counter-hegemonic discourse that works to destabilize hegemonic discourse. But this can be achieved without denying that it is a discourse or according it epistemological privilege.

Second, all of Harding's talk of "less false stories," "less partial and perverse accounts," and more "objective" research necessarily presupposes a means by which the "less false," "less partial," and more objective can be distinguished from their alternatives. Yet it is unclear from Harding's account how this might be done. The centerpiece of Harding's critique of masculinist science is her rejection of the metanarrative that grounds this science and her denial of the very possibility of such a metanarrative. Given this rejection and this denial, the mechanism by which Harding's "less false stories" will be recognized as such is confused. Obviously, the masculinist discourse of science is unlikely to label feminist claims as "less partial and perverse" than their own accounts. On the contrary, the scientific establishment has devoted much effort to discrediting the validity of feminist claims. If Harding rejects the existing metanarrative of the scientific establishment and argues that we should not construct a rival metanarrative, then it is incumbent on her to provide a detailed epistemological explanation of how we distinguish among different accounts of "reality." But she does not provide such an explanation.

What I identify as Harding's dilemma, however, is far from unique. It highlights a problem that is central to what I am calling the third strategy of feminist theory. If feminists seek to challenge the hegemonic discourse of modernity in science, epistemology, or any other area, their strategic options are few. If they counter the absolutism and universality of this discourse with another absolutist and universalist metanarrative, they incur all the epistemological liabilities of that discourse. Further, their arguments will most likely be dismissed as nonsensical, because there is no common ground between the two rival metanarratives. If they attempt to operate within the hegemonic discourse, however, they risk co-optation and jeopardize the possibility of significant change. Harding's dilemma illustrates the need for feminists to find a way to negotiate these issues if they are to define a new epistemological space for feminist theory.[12]

Toward a new paradigm

When feminist standpoint theory emerged in the late 1970s, it appeared to be exactly what the feminist movement needed: a method for naming the oppression of women grounded in the truth of women's lives. Standpoint theory constituted a challenge to the masculinist definition of truth and method embodied in the dominant modernist discourses of science and epistemology. It established an alternative vision of truth and, with it, hope for a less repressive society. But the theoretical tensions implicit in the theory soon came to the forefront. The contradiction between social constructionist and absolutist conceptions of truth haunted both versions of the theory. In Hartsock's philosophical version it was translated into the dichotomy between the truth of women's material condition and abstract masculinity; in the sociological version it was translated into the dichotomy between "women's experience" and abstract sociological categories. Both these formulations ultimately proved untenable. As the theory developed in the late 1980s and early 1990s, questions of how feminists should theorize differences among women and the status of feminism's truth claims became impossible to ignore – and equally impossible to answer within the confines of the original theory.

Feminist standpoint theory was originally conceived as an alternative vision of truth and reality, a replacement for what Hartsock calls abstract masculinity. The intent of the foregoing has been to illustrate that the theoretical legacy of feminist standpoint theory has been not to establish such an alternative, but, rather, to call into question the viability of totalizing visions. Because of the dualistic conception of truth and reality that characterized its original formulation, feminist standpoint theory has had the effect not of establishing an alternative truth but of problematizing absolutes and universals, focusing attention on the situated, local, and communal constitution of knowledge. Another way of putting this is that in attempting to interpret feminist standpoint theory we should look to Kuhn, not Marx. Feminist standpoint theory is part of an emerging paradigm of knowledge and knowledge production that constitutes an epistemological break with modernism. Feminist standpoint theory defines knowledge as particular rather than universal; it jettisons the neutral observer of modernist epistemology; it defines subjects as constructed by relational forces rather than transcendent. As feminist standpoint theory has developed, the original tension between social construction and universal truth has begun to dissolve. But it is significant that this has been accomplished not by privileging one side of the dichotomy but by deconstructing the dichotomy itself. The new paradigm of knowledge toward which feminist standpoint theory is moving involves rejecting the definition of knowledge and truth as *either* universal *or* relative in favor of a conception of all knowledge as situated and discursive.

One of the ways of illustrating this shift is to return to an analysis of the work of Sandra Harding. In her 1986 book, Harding distinguishes between feminist standpoint theory and feminist post-modernism on the grounds that the former claims a privileged epistemic position while the latter does not. She argues that a notion of "truth" that is not relative to social constructions is a necessary element of feminist theory and, for this reason, rejects the validity of feminist postmodernism. If we look at this distinction in Harding's 1991 book, however, we find a very different story. There she advocates what she calls a "postmodernist standpoint approach." She focuses on one of the major themes of feminist standpoint theory – that knowledge is situated in the material lives of social actors – and uses it to unite what she had identified, a mere five years before, as distinct strands of feminist theory. Most significantly, the major distinction between postmodernism and standpoint theory – the claim of privileged knowledge and one, true reality has been almost entirely abandoned.

As the foregoing analysis indicates, Harding is not the only contemporary feminist standpoint theorist who has significantly modified the claim to privileged knowledge. Hartsock's work illustrates a similar pattern. Ruddick never advanced a claim to privileged knowledge. Flax, an early proponent of the feminist standpoint, has enthusiastically embraced postmodernism and the multiple truths it entails. The notion of a feminist standpoint that is truer than previous (male) ones, she now claims, rests on problematic and unexamined assumptions (1990: 56).[13] What these theorists are effecting is a version of Code's "remapping of the epistemic terrain." What is significant about this remapping, however, is that for all these theorists, defining reality as socially constructed and multiple does not obviate but, rather, facilitates critical analysis.

The feminist theorist who has done the most to define what I am calling the new paradigm of truth and method is Donna Haraway. The aspect of her work that speaks most directly to feminist standpoint theory is her well-known essay "A manifesto for cyborgs" (1990). Haraway states her goal in the article as attempting to build "an ironic political myth faithful to feminism, socialism and materialism" (1990: 190). Haraway identifies the central element of this myth as the "cyborg": "I am making an argument for the cyborg as a fiction mapping our social and bodily reality and as an imaginative resource suggesting some fruitful couplings" (1990: 191). The cyborg, she claims, is our ontology; it gives us our politics. It "is a condensed image of both imagination and material reality, the two joined centers structuring any possible historical transformation" (1990: 191).

I would like to suggest that Haraway's aim in this article is an attempt to refashion feminist standpoint theory so that it is compatible with what I am calling the new paradigm of knowledge. The central element of that refashioning is Haraway's attack on the concept of "women's experience." This concept is the foundation of feminist standpoint theory, the unquestioned ground on which it rests. Haraway argues that this ground is ungrounded. The women's movement, she claims, has *constructed* "women's experience"; it is not a given. Rather, "This experience is a fiction and a fact of the most crucial, political kind" (1990: 191).

Haraway's goal here is principally to reject essentializing moves in feminist theory. But her argument goes beyond mere negation to a positive theory of concept formation. Feminist standpoint theory, she claims, is essentialist, in that its epistemology is based on the ontological structure of women's labor (1990: 200). Against this she argues that women's experience is constructed. Like every other aspect of our lives, it is apprehended through concepts that are of our making. This is where the cyborg comes in. The cyborg is a constructed concept, but it is *our* constructed concept. Women constructed the notion of "women's experience" because the concepts of masculinist science made the experiences of women invisible. The construction of "women's experience" was thus necessary in order to bring women's reality into the purview of science. But Haraway's point is that it was not necessary to essentialize and ontologize this concept. Instead, she claims that we should regard women's experience as both a fictitious concept *and* a political fact. Women's experience is not an absolute, a given, but a construct with important political implications for feminism.

The cyborg is Haraway's replacement for the flaws of "women's experience." "The cyborg is resolutely committed to partiality, irony, intimacy, and perversity. It is oppositional, utopian, and completely without innocence" (1990: 192). It is not structured by polarities but, on the contrary, displaces them. Most important, it displaces the reality/appearance polarity on which feminist standpoint theory rests. It is, Haraway argues, exactly the kind of concept that feminists need. It is avowedly constructed; it makes no claim to apprehend totalities or essences. It is also avowedly political; unlike the "scientific" concepts of both masculinist science and Marxism, it declares its lack of innocence and objectivity; it was constructed for a specific political purpose – feminist politics. Finally, it is transformative: it has the potential to "transgress boundaries." Haraway argues: "So my cyborg myth is about transgressed boundaries, potent fusions and dangerous possibilities which progressive people might explore as one part of needed political work" (1990: 196). The "cyborg politics" that she defines is a struggle against "one code" that translates all meaning perfectly (1990: 218). Feminist standpoint theory told us that women occupy a privileged epistemological position because they are closer to the "ground of life." Against this, Haraway argues that "the production of universal, totalizing theory is a major mistake that misses most of reality." She concludes that what we need instead is a "powerful infidel heteroglossia" (1990: 223).

In another context Haraway summarizes these points:

> There is no single feminist standpoint because our maps require too many dimensions for that metaphor to ground our visions. But the feminist standpoint theorists' goal of an epistemology and politics of engaged, accountable positioning remains eminently potent. The goal is better accounts of the world, that is, "science." (1988: 590)

What I have identified as Haraway's refashioning of feminist standpoint theory reveals the strengths of the theory – the emphasis on situated and perspectival knowledge – while avoiding its commitment to essentialism and totality. In the last sentence of this passage, however, Haraway moves her critique to another level. If, as Haraway and other critics of feminist standpoint theory argue, we amend the theory to accommodate multiple standpoints, the social construction of "reality," and the necessity of an engaged political position, how can we talk about "better accounts of the world," "less false stories"? And indeed, how we can talk about accounts of the world at all if the multiplicity of standpoints is, quite literally, endless? These questions are also an important legacy of feminist standpoint theory. My principal goal in tracing the evolution of feminist standpoint theory has been to emphasize that this evolution was, in some sense, inevitable. Once feminist standpoint theorists began discussing the social construction of reality and knowledge, it was only a matter of time before the privileged status of knowledge implicit in feminist standpoint theory would be challenged. But I also want to emphasize that the deconstruction of the absolutism of feminist standpoint theory points to a crucially important challenge facing contemporary feminist theory: defining a new epistemological space for feminism.

The central aspect of this challenge is defining "science." As several decades of feminist critiques of science have revealed, this is no easy task. Masculinist science, like early feminist standpoint theory, demands epistemic privilege, a point from which the "truth" of reality can be revealed. Although feminist standpoint theory represents an attempt to duplicate that epistemic privilege, it also reveals its liability. The attempt to define "women's material reality," "women's experience," or "women's labor" as the absolute ground for truth claims about the oppression of women caused serious problems for feminist standpoint theory. But the history of that theory also reveals the difficulty of challenging the epistemology of masculinist science. If we concede that no perspective is privileged, that all are partial, then we must redefine what science is all about; we must redefine a "better account" without appealing to an absolute grounding.

For feminism, redefining science must involve defining concepts that can "see" the world from a different perspective. As the feminist standpoint theorists so clearly illustrated, women's experience is quite literally invisible to masculinist science. Thus it is necessary to develop new, feminist concepts that can describe women's experience and fashion it into a feminist science. This is what feminist standpoint theorists did so brilliantly in their analyses. Another step in this redefinition is convincing nonfeminists that these accounts are, in Haraway's words, "better accounts of the world, that is, science." This involves transgressing boundaries, redefining some of the basic parameters of the hegemonic discourse of science, so that feminist science, can be defined as "true."

These tasks are the subject of the rest of this book. Although my focus is methodological and epistemological, politics is an inseparable aspect of my argument. As I argued in chapter 1, the paradigm shift now under way demands a new definition of politics as well as a new definition of truth. Politics and epistemology, as the history of feminist standpoint theory so clearly illustrates, are necessarily intertwined: we act politically on the basis of what we claim to be true. My goal is to clarify the truth claims of what I am calling the third strategy of feminist theory; this will involve, at the same time, defining the parameters of its politics.[14]

3

A Method for Differences

Feminism, method, and difference

In an article that appeared in Nicholson's 1990 collection *Feminism/
Postmodernism*, Susan Bordo calls for an examination of an issue
that she identifies as the most vexing problem in contemporary
feminist theory: how feminist method can accommodate difference.
How, she asks, can feminists theorize difference without losing the
analytic force of gender analysis? In a highly nuanced and sophisticated analysis, Bordo addresses what she calls the "gender skepticism" of recent feminist theory. She defends gender analysis as a
valuable and indispensable tool for feminist theorizing while at the
same time acknowledging that feminist theory must be able to
accommodate differences of race, class, and historical particularity.
Although she refers to the influences of postmodernism and poststructuralism in her analysis, Bordo makes it clear that this is not her
only concern. The question, she claims, is not whether feminism
should embrace postmodernism but, rather, how feminists can theorize difference without abandoning the advantages of the generalizing
perspective of gender analysis.

Bordo's analysis of the dilemma of difference facing feminist theory is both incisive and disturbing. She reveals the central issues at
stake in the dilemma and the difficulty of formulating a solution. She
acknowledges that feminist theory must be sensitive to the differences
among women and how those differences constitute different realities

for variously situated women. But she also points out that attention to differences problematizes systemic analysis, analysis that must, of necessity, reconstitute or even ignore some of those differences. Postmodernism, poststructuralism, and deconstruction, she argues, have induced feminists to abandon generalizations a priori and to define gender as textual play. The "invaluable insight" of these approaches, she claims, is that "gender forms only one axis of a complex, heterogeneous construction, constantly interpenetrating, in historically specific ways, with multiple other axes of identity" (1990: 139). Bordo nevertheless argues strongly against the "gender skepticism" these approaches have fostered. She advances two arguments in defense of gender analysis. First, she asserts that the "gender theorists" – most notably Gilligan, Dinnerstein, and Chodorow – discovered patterns that "resonate experientially and illuminate culturally"; they "described a new territory" (1990: 137). Second, she questions what she sees to be the alternative to gender analysis: the proliferation of differences. She asks, "just how many axes *can* one include and still preserve analytic focus or argument?" (1990: 139). No matter how attentive we are as scholars, some axes of identity will inevitably be ignored, others selected; we see from points of view that are invested with our social and political interests (1990: 140). She concludes that feminists today are less in danger of the totalizing theories feared by the gender skeptics than by increasing paralysis at the fear of being essentialist (1990: 142).

In terms of the analysis that I have developed here, what Bordo is asking is how we can move to a new paradigm that focuses on differences without losing one of the principal advantages of the second strategy: the gender analysis facilitated by the emphasis on difference. I agree with Bordo that this question is fundamental to the future of feminist theory. If the paradigm of differences precludes any discussion of gender as a general category or, for that matter, any general categories at all, then it is seriously deficient. It will thwart rather than foster the development of feminist theory. One way of restating Bordo's question is to ask whether we are throwing out the baby of general analysis with the bathwater of the second strategy. Her argument, that we must choose *some* axes of analysis and reject others, or our arguments will devolve into trivialities about individual women, is both irrefutable and profoundly disturbing. If we emphasize only the differences among women, we will be unable to rise above the infinity of differences. If differences become, in a sense, the new absolute, then we have no basis on which to justify or even formulate general analytic categories. Defining the paradigm of differences as precluding the elision of any differences makes any such categories illegitimate. Bordo's argument is that an absolute commitment to differences eliminates the use of the general category that has been so central to feminist theorizing: gender. But her point applies as well to any other concept that elides differences among women.

The problem of how to articulate a method for differences has been at the forefront of feminist theory in the past decade. A number of feminists have attempted to answer this challenge by claiming that we are, indeed, throwing the baby out with the bathwater and thus must return to at least a quasi-universalism. Martha Nussbaum's polemical article in *Political Theory* set the stage for this approach. Nussbaum is disturbed by her perception that people who identify themselves as progressives – feminists, anti-racists, etc. – are taking up positions that converge with reaction, oppression, and sexism (1992: 204). The reason, she claims, is that the retreat into extreme relativism or even subjectivism leaves these theorists unable to evaluate social practices. She asserts that this tendency turns us over to "the free play of forces" in a world in which the situation of non-hegemonic groups is disadvantageous (1992: 212). The solution she poses is "historically informed essentialism." She argues that we can identify basic human functions that give us the foundation from which to judge social and political institutions – what she calls a "thick, vague theory of the good" (1992: 214). Based on her perception that there is a "great convergence across cultures" on human values, Nussbaum supplies a list of the "shape of the human form of life." The list, she claims, is both evaluative and "internal to human history" (1992: 223).

Nussbaum's sentiments are echoed by several other theorists. Jane Martin asserts that feminism's determination to honor diversity among women and, thus, eschew generalizations has lead to the "stunting" of intellectual inquiry (1994: 631). What Martin calls "compulsory historicism" has, she argues, deprived feminism of the general concepts that have served us well in the past. Echoing Bordo's fears, Martin wonders how we can handle all the diversities that we are discovering among women. Her solution is to use categories that uncover the differences we regard as the most important. Two other authors, Judith Kay (1994) and Susan Moller Okin (1994) address the political implications of the anti-essentialist trend. Kay argues that successful political coalitions require a "substantial concept of common humanity grounded in an explicit notion of human nature" (1994: 21). Like Nussbaum, she supplies a long list of "human capacities" that can ground our discourse on human nature. Okin takes a more empirical tack, arguing that the anti-essentialist arguments made by feminists are not convincing. Examining the validity of the claim that there is a generalizable, identifiable, collective experience of women, she answers with a qualified "yes." She concludes that "gender itself is an extremely important category of analysis and that we ought not be paralyzed by the fact that there are differences among women" (1994: 20).[1]

The arguments of these theorists have the tone of a backlash: a reaction against a popular trend through appeal to a previous mode of thought. They are trying to recapture the advantages of a disappearing paradigm rather than attempting to redefine these elements in a new paradigm. It would not be difficult to argue that this approach is methodologically flawed – that is, that the list of human universals which these authors identify is based on reports of other cultures by Western scholars and thus reflects Western – not universal – values. But there is also an epistemological problem implicit in this approach. In her critique of the anti-essentialists, Nussbaum argues that they espouse precisely the metaphysical realism that they claim to debunk; that is, they assume that if there are no absolutes or universals, then the only alternative is "extreme relativism." I agree. Many of the advocates of differences assume that all general categories, as well as the possibility of evaluation, are obviated by their position. But Nussbaum herself falls prey to this assumption. She assumes that without at least a modified conception of universal human nature, the possibility of any generalities or evaluation is precluded.[2] She thus sees the challenge of theory as defining a historically informed essentialism. Her strategy is to define universals and then qualify them historically and culturally. I think this strategy is backwards. Against the essentialists, I argue that we should start with historically and culturally situated women and develop both specific and general categories by which we can evaluate their social reality. Against both the essentialists and the extreme anti-essentialists, I believe that we can both justify general concepts and make moral judgments, and that we can do so without appealing to absolutes and universals. But I also believe that this requires a detailed epistemological argument that neither Nussbaum nor the anti-essentialists have supplied.

Important elements of just such an epistemological argument, however, have emerged in the work of contemporary feminist epistemologists and feminist philosophers of science. My goal is to build on these epistemologies and, specifically, to develop an aspect of the epistemological problem that has been overlooked: a feminist approach to the social sciences. The work of four contemporary feminist theorists has been the most significant: Helen Longino, Lorraine Code, Sandra Harding, and Lynn Hankinson Nelson. Although there are significant differences among these theorists, and each, to a greater or lesser degree, breaks away from modernist epistemology, there is a common impulse informing their work: defining knowledge as situated and social without abandoning the systemic analysis that is definitive of "science." This impulse takes different forms: negotiating the relative/absolute dichotomy, accommodating difference while retaining general concepts, redefining objectivity and evidence. But in all cases the goal of defining an epistemology that transcends the dichotomies of modernism is paramount. In the following I borrow heavily from the work of these theorists. But I also argue that several important issues are inadequately explored in their work, and, most significantly for my concerns, that they pay little attention to the social sciences.

In *Science as Social Knowledge* (1990) Helen Longino declares that her goal is to show how social values play a role in scientific research. Note that she says "how," not "whether." From the first pages of her book, Longino makes it clear that she is attempting to formulate a new definition of science, a science in which the influence of values is not equated with "bad" science. The crux of her argument is her assertion that a value-free or autonomous science is neither methodologically possible nor desirable; it puts unrealistic constraints on the activity of science (1990: 13). Against this she argues that science is socially created: it is social in the process of creation as well as the uses it serves (1990: 75–6).

Longino is acutely aware that such a sweeping redefinition of science incurs serious problems. Specifically, it calls for redefinitions of rationality and objectivity, definitions that include rather than exclude values. Informing this discussion and, indeed, most of the feminist critiques of science, is a very specific fear: if we abandon rationality and objectivity as they have been defined by modernist (masculinist) science, we will sink into "unbridled relativism." Longino, like many other feminist theorists, is concerned to avoid that alternative by redefining these concepts so that they retain some semblance of their former status. Her way of doing so is to define objectivity as the practice of a community rather than of individuals. The advantage of this definition for Longino is that it retains the distinction between objectivity and subjectivity. A social concept of objectivity, she argues, minimizes the influence of subjective preferences. If science is to provide knowledge, rather than a random collection of opinions, subjective preferences must be held at bay (1990: 216). A concept of objectivity based on a community's values is her means of accomplishing this goal.

The result of Longino's redefinition of objectivity is what she calls "contextual empiricism": what we experience at any given time can be measured in conventional ways (1990: 221). Experience is a product of the interaction of our senses, our conceptual apparatus, and the "world out there"; it is a function of what aspects of the world out there we choose to interact with, which aspects our intellectual commitments direct us toward (1990: 221). She concludes: "While eschewing the concept of a single truth or hope of a singular epistemological blessing, we can nevertheless rank theories as to their acceptability, in particular their worthiness as bases for collective action to solve common problems" (1990: 214).

Longino's theory goes a long way toward the remapping of the epistemic domain that feminists are seeking. Her distinction between the objectivity established by a scientific community and the subjective preferences of individuals is valuable and insightful. This argument is crucial to establishing an alternative to the "view from nowhere" on one hand and individual variation on the other. But some significant questions remain, particularly if Longino's theory is applied to the social sciences. First, all her discussions of "community" sidestep the question of the constitution of that community. What Longino's analysis comes to is the revelation that, for all these years, the bastion of masculinist science has told us that scientific knowledge is autonomous and value-free, and now we are discovering that it is, rather, communal knowledge based on the specific values that constitute that community. This scores a significant epistemological point, but, in practical terms, still leaves feminists out in the cold. It is still *their* community and it is still by *their* standards (now defined as conventional rather than objective) that knowledge is defined. Second, Longino's contextual empiricism, which defines an interaction among our senses, our conceptual apparatus, and the "world out there," only explains the situation of the natural sciences. In the social sciences the "world out there" is an already constituted world, a world constituted by the concepts of social actors. These concepts, furthermore, are frequently hostile to women. Even more significantly, masculinist social science has not, until very recently, included conceptual tools that can grasp and analyze those aspects of social reality that constitute "women's reality." In order to grasp that reality, feminists must develop a new conceptual apparatus and incorporate it into the existing social-scientific disciplines. In short, we need another level of epistemological explanation specific to the problems of the social sciences.

In *What Can She Know?* (1991) Lorraine Code takes a more aggressive stance against the bastion of masculinist science. Instead of redefining objectivity, she asserts that the objective/subjective dichotomy no longer holds. Code cuts a broad swath through the epistemological terrain of modernist knowledge. She defines a perspectival, situated knowledge in both epistemology and moral theory, arguing against the "autonomous knower" of the modernist tradition. She defines knowledge as both subjective and objective: subjective in that "it is marked, as product, by the processes of its construction by specifically located subjects; objective in that the construction process is constrained by a reality that is recalcitrant to inattentive or whimsical structurings" (1991: 255). Like Longino, Code wants to avoid subjectivism. Her solution is what she calls "regulative realism."

Unlike Longino, however, Code takes on the question of women's relationship to the social as well as the natural sciences. Specifically, she addresses the role of ideology in the definition of women's place in the social order. She argues that women must be able to "fight science with science" – that is, to both resist the scientific community's definition of women and formulate alternative knowledges (1991: 219). This is a significant step. It is essential if women are to resist the scientific community's definition of knowledge and, specifically, its definition of knowledge about women. Code then deals with the difficult question of how this can be accomplished if women are excluded from the construction of knowledge. First, she argues, "women can learn, collectively, to give and withhold acknowledgment and hence to claim power for their knowledge" (1991: 219). Second, they can tap the "recessive resources" that exist in any discursive formation. No discourse, she asserts, is so homogeneous that it cannot be changed (1991: 220).

One of the most significant aspects of Code's analysis is her discussion of a book that has come to represent the paradigm case of constructing women's knowledge: *Women's Ways of Knowing* (Belenky et al. 1986). The authors of this book attempt to define distinctively feminine ways of knowing rooted in the experiences of women. Basing their analysis on extensive interviews with women, the authors define five "women's ways of knowing" that derive from these experiences, ways of knowing that are denigrated by masculinist definitions of knowledge. The message of the book is that women should acknowledge and valorize these ways of knowing, holding them up as equal to the hegemonic (masculinist) definition of knowledge.

Code rejects the approach of *Women's Ways of Knowing* on the grounds that we must maintain a distinction between knowledge and experience. Experience, she claims, is a narrative without conclusions or analysis. She argues that what we need, by contrast, is knowledge – a critical interpretation of the "real world," not just the stories of women; our conception of knowledge must include subjective knowledge, but not subjectivism (1991: 255–6). Code's argument against subjective experience here parallels Longino's argument against "unbridled relativism." In both cases there is an attempt to shore up the defenses against an approach in which "anything goes." Longino appeals to the "world out there." Code's appeal is more tenuous. She appeals to a world resistant to "whimsical structurings"; she advocates a "mitigated relativism constrained by objectivity and a commitment to realism" (1991: 251).

Closely related to the problem of subjectivism is the problem of differences. "A central tension in present-day feminist thought," Code argues, is "the problem of how to take women's differences and specificities adequately into account while retaining and extending the power to speak with political cohesiveness *about* and *for* women" (1991: 259). We can accomplish this, Code argues, by doing without an epistemological theory, opening up critical possibilities, remapping the epistemic terrain into numerous, fluid conversations (1991: 306–9). I agree with all but one aspect of this diagnosis and solution. Feminism must learn to accommodate differences without losing the ability to construct knowledge about women and formulate a feminist politics. But it is erroneous – even dangerous – to conclude that this entails abandoning epistemological theory.[3] I think it entails, on the contrary, the necessity to formulate an alternative epistemology that precisely and explicitly justifies and legitimizes the "numerous fluid conversations" that Code envisions. We must formulate an epistemology that, particularly in the social sciences, intersects with the hegemonic epistemology of those disciplines in ways that can transform them from within. Code begins this task but does not fill in the crucial details that are necessary for its completion.

Sandra Harding's *Whose Science? Whose Knowledge?* (1991), like Code's book, addresses the broad epistemological questions raised by feminism's relationship to science. In the previous chapter I discussed Harding's approach to feminist standpoint theory and identified what I see to be the liabilities of that approach. These liabilities extend to the entirety of Harding's theory. Harding begins her book with the assertion that her goal is not to resolve all the tensions and contradictions between feminism and Western models of science, but to "advance more useful ways for us to think about and plan their future encounters. The truth (whatever that is!) cannot set us free. But less partial and less distorted beliefs – less false beliefs – are a crucial resource for understanding ourselves and others, and for designing liberatory social relations" (1991: xi). This brief statement reveals the main themes that Harding develops in her book – themes that, I think, reveal tensions and contradictions internal to her own position.

The first theme is revealed in Harding's reference to "future encounters." Harding argues that feminism cannot simply reject the scientific tradition whole hog. Rather, she asserts that feminists must "encounter" science, both on its own terms and in an effort to alter those terms. The second theme emerges in the phrase "less partial and less distorted beliefs." Harding wants to argue simultaneously that the single, universal truth of science is an illusion and that we can and should distinguish between more or less false beliefs. Third, Harding's reference to "liberatory social relations" reveals her attempt to link science and politics and her rejection of the elitism and autonomy of the scientific tradition.

The tensions among these three themes emerge as Harding develops her arguments. In order to accomplish the goal of planning the future encounters of feminism and science, Harding must first address the second theme, defining the distinction between more and less false beliefs. She begins by asserting that scientific rationality is not all bad, but, rather, that Western science contains both progressive and regressive tendencies: "The very scientific rationality that has been the object of criticism in so many quarters contains the resources for its own transformation" (1991: 10). Harding's development of this thesis, however, produces a kind of bifurcated consciousness in her account. On one hand, Harding sounds very much like the radical critics of scientific rationality. She labels her position the "postmodernist" standpoint approach, to distinguish it from the modernist Marxist version. She argues that feminist reflections on scientific knowledge challenge the dominant epistemology of science. Harding's statements in guarded defense of the epistemology of science however, counter these radical tendencies. Her postmodernist feminist standpoint theory does not simply reject the epistemology of science but is, rather, "committed to rethinking and revising some important notions from conventional metatheories of science"

(1991: 49). Significantly, in order to accomplish this goal, Harding turns to the feminist epistemology most congruent with the epistemology of science: feminist empiricism. Far from rejecting feminist empiricism, she argues that it contains a radical potential. Many of the claims emerging from feminist empiricist research, she asserts, are true, or at least less false than those they oppose. Its radical potential lies in its ability to point beyond the epistemology of empiricism.

The point of Harding's guarded defense of empiricism and the rationality of Western science emerges most clearly in her discussion of postmodernism/poststructuralism. Contrasting poststructuralist critiques to that of feminist empiricism, Harding argues that poststructuralist critiques are unlikely to satisfy policymakers who want to know "how the world is" (1991: 304). Feminist empiricism, on the other hand, is a "conservative justificatory strategy" that is more acceptable to the scientific establishment (1991: 114), principally because it stresses continuity with the scientific tradition (1991: 136).

What this comes down to is that Harding advocates an internal transformation of science, rather than an external revolution, on the grounds that this will be the most effective strategy for changing masculinist science. She summarizes her strategy in the phrase "the outsider within." It is important, she asserts, to work and think outside the dominant modes, but it is also important "to bring the insights developed there into the heart of conventional institutions, to disrupt the dominant practices from within by appropriating notions such as objectivity, reason and science in ways that stand a chance of compelling reasoned assent while simultaneously shifting and displacing the meanings and referents to the discussion in ways that improve it" (1991: 160).

I could not agree more. Harding's stated strategy for transforming science is, I think, the only viable one. She expresses what I see to be the paradoxical situation of feminist theory: unless we cast arguments in terms that can be judged "reasonable" by the scientific establishment, these arguments will have little chance of accomplishing the feminist goal of transformation. But I am not convinced that Harding has given us an outline of such a strategy. Her discussion of "strong objectivity" is a case in point. Although Harding's use of the term "objectivity" would seem to indicate that she wants to retain some elements of the hegemonic concept, this is not, in fact, the case. Harding makes it clear that her definition of objectivity rests on the social situatedness of all knowledge – what she calls "historical relativism" (1991: 156). This is not a concept of objectivity recognizable in the hegemonic discourse of science. But Harding does not leave it at this. She asserts that some social situations generate more objective knowledge claims than others, and that the means to achieving such objectivity is starting research in "women's lives" (1991: 142–50). This is where the feminist standpoint comes in. If all knowledge is socially situated, then some social situations will yield more objective knowledge claims than others. This explains Harding's claim that starting research in the lives of the most oppressed women will yield the most objective claims (1991: 179–80). Finally, Harding claims that the kind of scientific research that she advocates would erase the distinction between subjects and objects of knowledge, that both researcher and researched would be placed in the same causal plane as objects of knowledge (1991: 11).

Harding's argument here is confusing on a number of levels. Her definition of "strong objectivity" as social situatedness is the antithesis of the hegemonic concept. Yet, what she takes away with one hand, she gives back with the other. The objectivity of knowledge claims, she asserts, can be guaranteed by starting research in "women's lives." This is dangerous territory for the feminist critique of science. One of the crucial aspects of the feminist critique is the argument (one that Harding herself espouses) that all knowledge is socially constituted. Thus feminists have rejected the "view from nowhere" that defines objectivity in the hegemonic discourse of science. "Starting research in women's lives," however, has all the trappings of the "view from nowhere." It is a "given" realm of empirical facts on which objective knowledge can rest. Further, Harding's advocacy of erasing the distinction between subject and object of knowledge is also problematic. For someone who wants to retain a notion of "science" and to distinguish between more and less objective accounts, this strategy is counterproductive. Although we must redefine subjects and objects in the transformed science we are seeking, erasing the distinction altogether erases the activity of science itself by making it indistinguishable from social action.

Harding's goal of transforming science through the "outsider within" offers a useful model for feminist critiques of science. It is the model that I follow in my discussion of feminist social science. But Harding's concrete suggestions for how this transformation should take place are less useful. She bounces back and forth between radical critiques of science on one hand and carefully circumscribed modifications of that discourse on the other. She adopts the postmodern label and endorses elements of postmodernism's radical critique of science. But she also argues that postmodernism cannot tell us "how the world is" and consequently turns to a redefined empiricism as a superior justificatory strategy. Finally, she concludes with an appeal to a new objectivity: "women's lives." I think that this is the wrong direction for feminist theory. Instead of trying to tell less false or less partial stories and grounding our distinctions in the objectivity of social reality, we should develop an epistemology that acknowledges the partiality of all stories and formulate arguments in defense of the stories we find to be useful for feminism. It is only by defining such an epistemology that we can fulfill Harding's goal of transforming science.

Another feminist theorist who does not want to reject the scientific tradition entirely is Lynn Hankinson Nelson. In *Who Knows?* (1990) Nelson focuses feminist attention on the issue of empiricism, arguing that feminists' rejection of empiricism is based on false assumptions about evidence in scientific reasoning. In order to develop an approach to empiricism that is compatible with feminism, Nelson turns to the work of Quine. The Quinian thesis that becomes the centerpiece of her approach is that it is communities, not individuals, that acquire knowledge. Quine, Nelson argues, defines a position between radical social constructionism and a passive view of knowledge acquisition. While rejecting the possibility of any pre-theoretical knowledge of the world, Quine nevertheless asserts that all evidence for science is sensory (Nelson 1990: 22).

Like Kuhn, Quine argues that science is a bridge between humans and nature, but it is "a bridge of our own making" (1990: 187). But Quine (and Nelson) diverge from Kuhn on the matter of evidence. Kuhn would have us believe that facts are constructed entirely by scientific theories. This leads, Nelson claims, to a denial of our commonsense sensory experience of the world. Following Quine, Nelson argues that Kuhn is wrong in portraying scientific communities as closed off from the rest of the world. Quine defines scientific communities as "without borders" – reflecting the commonsense understandings of the larger society (1990: 137). An important consequence of her view is Nelson's assertion that metaphysics is always embedded in science, that science always has political and social implications. Thus our commonsense understandings of the world, including our sensory experiences of that world, are embedded in scientific understandings; there is no clear line between them. For, Nelson argues, "in an important sense, just about everyone is an empiricist" (1990: 20).

Nelson uses the connection she has posited between science and commonsense to construct a bridge between the scientific and feminist communities. Many feminists reject empiricism because they assume that it presupposes the positivist view of objectivity and individualism. Nelson wants to replace this definition of empiricism with the Quinian definition of community-based knowledge. The result is that she can posit a "community" that includes feminists, nonscientists, and scientists. The beliefs and knowledge of this community, she declares, depend on public language and the conceptual schemes it embodies; what this community "knows" is constrained by public standards of evidence (1990: 256).[4] Nelson's conclusion is that although there is no pre-theoretical knowledge of the world, it is nevertheless the case that "the world matters" – that is, that sensory evidence is relevant to scientific theories.

Near the end of *Who Knows?* Nelson states that relativist epistemologies are inadequate because they do not allow us to distinguish between good and bad theories (1990: 294). What Nelson is proposing as an alternative is that we use empirical standards of evidence to make this distinction. She is able to make this argument compatible with feminist critiques of science by defining the scientific community as without borders: thus feminists and scientists are united by a commonsense empiricism. In short, Nelson hopes that both feminists and scientists can agree on what constitutes a "good" theory, because both can agree on what constitutes adequate evidence for a theory.

At the beginning of her book Nelson states that we must reopen the discussion between feminism and empiricism, because feminists must get empiricist scientists to listen if we are to change science (1990: 6). Harding made a similar argument in her work. Once more, I agree. I agree with Nelson that there are basic commonsense beliefs that provide the grounding for our form of life. I also agree that these beliefs provide a common understanding of the basic constitution of the natural world that informs investigations in the natural sciences. But I think that Nelson has left several important elements out of her equation. First, her formula does not work as well for the social sciences as it does for the natural sciences. The objects of investigation in the social sciences, unlike those in the natural sciences, are constituted by the concepts of social actors. The agreement that constitutes the social world is thus of a very different kind from that which constitutes the natural world. Even more significantly, the concepts that constitute the social world are not neutral with regard to women. On the contrary, they marginalize and silence women. Feminist social scientists, unlike their natural-scientific counterparts, are not merely trying to investigate this world. Their task, rather, is to create concepts that allow them to investigate the silenced world of women and hence change the constitution of that social world.

Second, Nelson's argument that we agree on what constitutes adequate evidence for a theory is problematic. Feminists have begun to change the standards for evidence in both the natural and the social sciences. Barbara McClintock's investigations accomplished, among other things, a change in what constitutes evidence for a "good" theory in biology. McClintock's method, gaining a "feeling for the organism," challenged both the methods and the definitions of adequate evidence in biological science (Keller 1983). This challenge is even more pronounced in the social sciences. Feminist social scientists have challenged both what constitutes a "fact" in their disciplines and what constitutes evidence for a "good" theory. When feminists began to enter the social sciences, they found that what they wanted to study was not conceptualized as an object of investigation in masculinist social science. Thus feminist social scientists created their own concepts and argued that the reality that these concepts portrayed was also a legitimate area of study in their disciplines. Introducing a new category of concepts entailed altering the parameters of the discipline, changing not only what constitutes a "fact" but also what constitutes evidence for a "good" theory pertaining to these facts.

An understanding of feminist social science, then, requires a different conception of the scientific community than that provided by Nelson. Feminist social science has produced fundamental changes in what counts as a "fact," a "proof," and "evidence" in their disciplines. But it is important to note that these changes, despite the fact that they have altered the parameters of the social-scientific disciplines, have been, in Harding's sense, effected by "outsiders within." The changes effected by feminist social scientists have been accepted because feminists have been successful in persuading their colleagues that feminist investigations are, and should be, a legitimate part of the social sciences. They did so by employing arguments that intersect with the dominant discourse of their disciplines, relying on common understandings of what constitutes a good argument while at the same time shifting those understandings.

Both Nelson and Harding believe that we must be able to distinguish between good and bad theories, more or less false accounts, in order to avoid "relativism." They both also agree that we must make arguments that make sense to the scientific community in order to transform it. My position is tangential to these arguments. I think that the concern with "relativism" is wrongheaded. It is my contention that one of the elements of the modernist/scientific paradigm that feminists must challenge is the notion that there are universal standards for good and bad theories. But I agree that feminists must cast their arguments in terms that are persuasive to the scientific establishment. We can do so, however, not because we share commonsense definitions of evidence, but because we share basic assumptions about what constitutes a good argument. These assumptions are not absolute or universal, but they are fundamental to what Wittgenstein calls our "form of life," what Weber calls the "general foundations of our orientation in the world." And, most significantly for the feminist project, they are malleable; their boundaries can be gradually shifted.

At the beginning of her essay "Dyke methods," Joyce Trebilcot states the three principles of her analysis: "First principle: I speak only for myself. Second principle: I do not try to get other wimmin to accept my beliefs. Third principle: There is no 'given'" (1988: 1). Trebilcot's solution to the problem of defining a feminist method is, I think, the problem rather than the solution. Trebilcot rails against the "truth industry" and even against other lesbians who make universal statements that "erase or misdescribe me" (1988: 2). As a solution, she wants to speak only for herself. Following Susan Bordo, I reject this as a blueprint for feminist method in the social sciences. If I can speak only for myself, my voice will have no effect; I might as well remain silent. If I cannot persuade others, or do not even try to, there is little point in speaking at all.

In the following I develop an epistemological grounding for a feminist method for the social sciences, a "method for differences" that both accommodates differences and justifies general concepts and categories. I think this effort is necessary for several reasons. The feminist critiques of science discussed above leave a number of crucial questions unanswered. These critiques concentrate on the natural sciences. The social sciences, where many of the key issues for feminism necessarily fall, have not received the careful epistemological analysis that feminists have devoted to the natural sciences. Feminist social science has generated unique problems that do not arise in the natural sciences. For example, there is a disturbing tendency among feminist social scientists to erect an absolute dichotomy between theory and experience and to argue for the necessity of the latter to the exclusion of the former. It is hard to imagine this as a problem in the natural sciences. Furthermore, values play a different role in the social and the natural sciences. Despite Quine's usefulness in developing a feminist empiricism, his absolute distinction between science and values disqualifies him as a guide for feminist social science. What feminist social science needs is a careful analysis of the multiple levels of intersection between social values and social science.

Feminist theorists have not, of course, ignored the social sciences in their attempts to refashion scientific reasoning. Feminist stand-point theory in particular was formulated as a distinctly feminist method for assessing social reality. But, as I argued in the previous chapter, this approach foundered on the problem of differences. Confronting the issue of differences and how to accommodate them has caused confusion in feminist approaches to social science. Although feminists have done insightful social-scientific research and continue to do so, no clear methodological alternative to the second strategy has emerged. It is my argument that we must develop a methodology to ground the third strategy. Specifically, we need to formulate an epistemological justification for feminist concepts in the social sciences that can accommodate differences while allowing and justifying systemic, general analysis.

In 1992 Shulamith Reinharz published a comprehensive overview of feminist methods in the social sciences. She begins the book with a quote from Dale Spender: "At the core of feminist ideas is the crucial insight that there is no one truth, no one authority, no one objective method which leads to the production of pure knowledge" (1992: 7). The descriptions of research methods that follow illustrate this maxim. The methods Reinharz describes emphasize difference and diversity; they focus on a variety of women's experiences; they deconstruct the rigid separation between observer and observed. What is missing, however, is any attempt to justify the truth claims made by the theorists who employ these methods. Spender is right: feminists reject the authority of "one truth." But the appeal to "one objective method" provided a justification for the truth claims that the method produced. If we reject this approach yet continue to make truth claims for the methods we employ, then we need another means of justifying and legitimizing those claims.

Various feminist philosophers have suggested ways in which we can provide such a legitimation. The recent work of Linda Nicholson (1994), Marilyn Frye (1992), Kathy Ferguson (1993), and Nancy Fraser (1995) offers perceptive commentaries on the problem of how to negotiate the problem of differences in feminist theory. Although these works are far from identical, they represent a grow-ing trend among feminist social and political theorists: the effort to define a form of social analysis that avoids the either/or of totalizing social critique on one hand and descriptions of individual experience on the other.[5] The most sustained attempt to develop such an approach is that of Iris Young. In *Justice and the Politics of Difference* Young introduces the notion of the "social group": "a collective of persons differentiated from at least one other group by cultural forms, practices, or ways of life" (1990: 43). The "politics of difference" that she develops in the book is defined in terms of this concept: social justice sometimes requires that certain groups receive special treatment. A central element of this politics is that group differences are relational, shifting; sometimes group differences will be more relevant, sometimes not (1990: 171).

Young's argument for the feminist use of relational and shifting categories of analysis is amplified in "Gender as seriality" (1994). Young's goal in this article is to fashion a feminist approach to social analysis that retains the advantages of the category "woman" without incurring its totalizing connotations. To accomplish this goal, Young turns to Sartre's concept of "seriality." For Sartre, seriality does not rest on the attribution of common identity and attributes, but on the structural relation to material objects as they have been produced and organized by a prior history; it is a vast, multifaceted, layered, and complex overlapping set of structures and objects (1994: 728). Defining women as a seriality, Young argues, has significant advantages. We can identify women as a collective without identifying common attributes that all women share. A series is unified passively by the objects around which their actions are oriented; women as a serial, thus, are "the individuals who are positioned as feminine by their activities surrounding those structures and objects" (1994: 728).

In her article Young asserts that a feminist theorist should be like a "Bandita," an intellectual outlaw raiding male philosophers' concepts for what she finds useful, leaving the rest behind (1994: 723). She advocates rejecting totalizing theory for a more pragmatic orientation. In what follows I am guided by both these maxims. Like Young, I look to a male theorist who can help me formulate a feminist method for social analysis. My goal in turning to Max Weber's work is not to replicate his theory but to raid it for feminist purposes. I am interested in Weber, furthermore, because his orientation as a social theorist is essentially pragmatic. Again and again he reiterates that, as social analysts, our overriding goal is to *understand* social reality; ultimately, it is this goal that justifies our concepts and orients our analysis. It is this aspect of his analysis that I employ as the basis for my project of defining a methodology for differences. I argue that the criterion that provides us with a means for deciding which concepts to apply in our analyses is not the truth of the social totality but, rather, the understanding of some particular aspect of social reality.

Weber's ideal type

Commenting on his use of Nietzsche's work, Foucault writes:

> For myself, I like to utilize the writers I like. The only valid tribute to thought such as Nietzsche's is precisely to use it, to deform it, to make it groan and protest. And if commentators say that I am being faithful or unfaithful to Nietzsche, that is of absolutely no interest. (1980: 53–4)

Using Weber's work for feminist purposes is an obvious example of making it "groan and protest" in Foucault's sense. Weber is in many respects a thoroughly masculinist/modernist writer (Bologh 1990). At the center of Weber's work is the rigidly individualistic definition of subjectivity that is the hallmark of modernity. For Weber it is the subject that is the focus of his attempt to explain how meaning is constituted in social reality; it is the subject who knows. Further, Weber's work is frequently associated with another hallmark of modernity: "objectivity." Many social-scientific textbooks define "objective social science" in terms of Weber's theory.

What makes it possible to turn his work to my purposes, however, is that, despite his modernist roots, Weber is a critic of some of the central tenets of modernism.[6] The hallmarks of modernity and the Enlightenment – rationalism, universality, presuppositionless objectivity, absolutism, and the effort to find the final truth about humans and their world – are all objects of Weber's critique; he casts doubt on the possibility of attaining any of these goals. As such, his method is at a tangent to Enlightenment rationalism and nomothetically conceived objective science (Green 1988: 281). Weber's attitude toward rationalism is, at best, an ambiguous one. Far from presupposing the universal validity of the concept, Weber's overriding question is why this particular form of thought and social organization arose in the West and nowhere else. His methodology is grounded in the rejection of the possibility of defining universal laws of human social life or grasping the totality of social reality. The central concept of his methodology, the ideal type, denies the possibility – or even the desirability – of formulating such universal laws. Ideal types define social analysis as necessarily one-sided and constituted by several levels of values.

It is even plausible to posit a similarity between Weber's work and that of some of the postmoderns, particularly Foucault. Like the postmoderns, Weber is centrally concerned with the "disenchantment" of the modern world. Weber's interest in Western rationalism is not rooted in the conviction of its rightness, but, rather, in the belief that we must cling to some form of knowledge against the void (Hennis 1988: 159). His question is how the West developed this unique form of knowledge and what consequences it entails. In the words of one theorist, "Weber is the Jeremiah of modern capitalism whose prophetic insight cannot be validated by the buttress of certain and reliable values" (B. Turner 1996: 354). For both Weber and the postmoderns the world is devoid of meaning; it becomes meaningful only through the meaning endowing of social actors. Although Weber approaches this situation very differently from, for example, Foucault, there are nevertheless significant similarities between the two (Hekman 1994; Gordon 1988; B. Turner 1988, 1996).

Weber fashioned the ideal type as a counter to the two positions that polarized the methodological dispute (*Methodenstreit*) of his day: the subjectivists on one hand and the advocates of a nomothetic social science on the other.[7] It is significant for my purposes that both these positions have parallels in contemporary methodological disputes, both feminist and nonfeminist.[8] The subjectivists of Weber's day claimed that the goal of social-scientific analysis is to minutely reproduce social reality through a process of intuiting or reliving the actions of social actors, a process in which no abstractions, laws, or concepts are employed. Against the subjectivists Weber argued that no aspect of social reality can be apprehended without presuppositions. In his words, "as soon as we attempt to reflect about the way in which life confronts us in immediate concrete situations, it presents an infinite multiplicity of successively and coexistently emerging and disappearing events" (1949: 72). Weber argues that we bring order to this multiplicity by relying on values, and, specifically, cultural values: "Order is brought into this chaos only on the condition that in every case only a *part* of concrete reality is interesting and *significant* to us, because only it is related to the *cultural values* with which we approach reality" (1949: 78). In another context Weber makes this point even more clearly: "The 'essence' of what happens [between social actors] is constituted by the 'meaning' which 'regulates' the course of their future conduct" (1977: 109).

Against the subjectivists, thus, Weber is arguing that even in every-day life we necessarily employ concepts and values to make sense of that life. We cannot enter into even the most rudimentary social encounters without reference to the concepts, presuppositions, values, and significance given to us as social actors. This activity is fundamental to human social life, not an aberrant and illegitimate activity of the social analyst. This point is crucial to Weber's discussion of how social scientists, as opposed to social actors, constitute their concepts. Weber's thesis is that the selection of the concepts of the social scientist is a two-step process, each involving a value choice. The first value choice is that imposed by the society in which the social scientist lives. The cultural values of a society impose an initial ordering of the multiplicity of possible meanings that confront social actors. Weber defines the second choice as individual rather than social: out of the set of cultural meanings the social scientist must choose an object of investigation. Weber argues that it is the investigator's individual values that guide this second selection: "without the investigator's evaluative ideas, there would be no principle of selection of subject-matter and no meaningful knowledge of the concrete reality" (1949: 82). The result of the investigator's choice is the conceptual tool that Weber calls the "ideal type":

> An ideal type is formed by the one-sided *accentuation* of one or more points of view and by the synthesis of a great many diffuse, discrete, more or less present and occasionally absent *concrete individual phenomena*, which are arranged according to one-sidedly emphasized viewpoints into a unified *analytic* construct. (1949: 90)

Weber's definition of the ideal type is a significant contribution to explaining how social scientists formulate analytic concepts. But it also raises a question: once the subject of analysis has been selected, how does the investigator know *which* elements to synthesize into the ideal type? Weber has little to say about this stage of the process of selection. He argues that "the most prominent and consequential of these features are selected and combined according to their compatibility" (1978a: 1111). The unity of the synthetic construct, he argues, "is constituted by the selection of those aspects which are 'essential' from the point of view of specific theoretical goals" (1975: 168). The key phrase here is "specific theoretical goals." Weber does not explicate this phrase but, rather, glosses over a complicated process that, I argue, should be defined as a third stage in the process of selecting objects of social analysis. This third stage is determined by the disciplinary matrix to which the social scientist adheres. This disciplinary matrix imposes two constraints on the construction of an ideal type. First, the concepts of the discipline define the appropriate objects of study in the social world. Each discipline defines what objects are worthy of study; aspects of social reality that are not conceptualized in the disciplinary matrix cannot become the object of investigation. Second, the disciplinary matrix also defines what Weber calls logical compatibility – that is, the rules by which the selected concepts are analyzed and assessed. What counts as "logical" analysis is thus, constituted by the disciplinary paradigms of the investigator's social-scientific community.

Weber almost entirely ignores the influence of what I identify as the third stage in the process of selecting analytic concepts. This is a significant lacuna in his theory, particularly for the analysis of feminist concepts. The influence of disciplinary matrices entails that social scientists can only study aspects of the social world that have been conceptualized by their discipline and deemed worthy of study. Further, they must analyze these concepts according to their discipline's definition of "logical" analysis. These are significant constraints. They entail that analyzing aspects of social reality not conceptualized and approved by the discipline or conducting analysis in what is defined as an "illogical" manner will result in "unscientific" results. These constraints establish the parameters of the discipline; what falls outside them does not count as "science."

When Weber moves on to a description of the role and functioning of ideal types, however, he is more precise. Ideal types are neither hypotheses nor descriptions of reality, but "yardsticks" by which reality can be compared; they are neither historical reality nor "true reality," but purely limiting concepts or "utopias"; the purpose of ideal types is to provide a means of comparison with concrete reality in order to reveal the significance of that reality (1949: 90–3); and, finally, ideal types serve as "a harbor until one has learned to navigate on the vast sea of empirical facts" (1949: 104). Although he is not as clear about it as he should be, the "reality" that Weber refers to in these passages is culturally constituted reality, not the "reality" of brute facts. What this entails is that the comparison that ideal types facilitate is between the social scientists' and the social actors' concepts. And the purpose of the comparison for the social scientist, as Weber reiterates, is to illuminate cultural reality. This is quite different from the presuppositionless assessment of brute social facts.

Weber's definition of the ideal type allows him to refute the positions of both the subjectivists and their opponents in the *Methoden-*

streit, the advocates of a nomothetic social science. Against the subjectivists Weber has shown that any understanding, even that of the most mundane social action, involves concepts and presuppositions; anticipating the postmoderns he even refers to the "discursive nature of our knowledge" (1949: 94). His point is that the social scientist's concepts, although distinct from those of the social actors, are built on those concepts and are, epistemologically, on a continuum with them. Weber can now use this argument against the subjectivists to refute their opponents' position as well. He argues against the advocates of a nomothetic social science that their assumption of a presuppositionless search for universal laws is false. All cultural analysis must begin with the values presupposed by cultural meaning. But Weber's principal argument against a nomothetic social science is that universal laws would fail to accomplish the purpose of social science: explaining the meaning of specific, unique events. Weber concludes that universal laws can reveal nothing about what social scientists want to explain: the significance of social phenomena. Ideal types, on the other hand, are specifically designed to do just that.

One of the most significant aspects of Weber's theory is that he did not define the ideal type as a new conceptual method but, rather, as an explication of existing social-scientific practice; ultimately, what Weber wanted to do was to explain what social scientists actually do. And what they do, he argues, is to probe the significance of unique events. This probing involves abstraction, but it is an abstraction that facilitates the understanding of social reality. Yet it is not the same kind of abstraction as that involved in the formation of universal laws. Unlike universal laws, ideal types cannot be refuted by contradictory cases; the discovery of contradictory cases reveals the irrelevance of the concept to the problem at hand, not its "error" (1975: 190). The "accuracy" of an ideal type thus rests on whether it explains the phenomenon under investigation, not whether it can be defined as a universal law.

Ideal types, Weber notes, are subject to continual change. In this they differ from the concepts of the nomothetic sciences and thus, it would seem, are inferior to those concepts. But Weber defines the changeability of ideal types as an asset rather than a liability (1949: 105, 159). Because of the unique relationship between ideal types and the values of both the society they conceptualize and the investigators who employ them, they will not remain constant. If the goal of the social sciences is the elucidation of the meaning of cultural reality, then this will be facilitated by the use of concepts specific to that society, not by reference to a universal schema. In an attempt to dispel the notion that the partial, changing nature of ideal-typical analysis is an indication of the inferiority of social-scientific method, a phase it will eventually transcend, Weber notes: "There are some sciences to which eternal youth is granted, and the historical disciplines are among them – all those to which the eternally onward flowing stream of culture perpetually brings new problems" (1949: 104). Clearly, Weber is battling the ghost of Plato here: the changing, the particular, is inferior to the eternal and the universal. It is an indication of Weber's movement into a new paradigm of thought that he holds his ground on this crucial issue. Since we must use ideal types in order to do social science, he argues, let us be clear about what it is we are doing by making our concepts unambiguous (1949: 43, 94).

It is Weber's understanding of the role of values in social-scientific analysis that informs his definition of the concept of objectivity in the social sciences. Weber did advocate "objectivity" in social science, but it is an objectivity so permeated by values that it bears only a passing resemblance to the modernist definition of objectivity. Weber defined ideal types as constituted by two sets of value presuppositions: the cultural significance endowed by the social scientist's society and the particular interest of the social-scientific investigator. Weber never deviates from his claim that ideal types are value-related in this dual sense. His definition of objectivity in his famous article on the subject does not deny this value-relatedness. Rather, he seeks to distinguish value-relatedness from value-judgments and to argue that it is the exclusion of value-judgments that provides the basis for objectivity.

This distinction is only one aspect of the ambiguity embedded in Weber's concept of objectivity. First, he concedes that the distinction between value-relatedness and value-judgments is difficult to make. Second, he wavers on the crucial issue of the status of the logic that guides scientific investigations. On one hand he seems to assert that this logic is universal. He states:

> It has been and remains true that a systematically correct scientific proof in the social sciences, if it is to achieve its purpose, must be acknowledged as correct even by a Chinese – or more precisely stated – it must constantly *strive* to attain this goal, which perhaps may not be completely attainable due to faulty data. Furthermore, the successful *logical* analysis of the content of an ideal and its ultimate axioms and the discovery of the consequences which arise from

pursuing it, logically and practically, must also be valid for the Chinese. (1949: 58)

Yet in the same context he qualifies this by asserting that "for even the knowledge of the most certain propositions of our theoretical science, e.g., the exact natural sciences or mathematics, is, like the cultivation and refinement of the conscience, a product of culture" (1949: 53). And similarly:

> All scientific work presupposes that the rules of logic and method are valid; these are the general foundations of our orientation in the world; and, at least for our special question, these presuppositions are the least problematic aspect of science. Science further presupposes that what is yielded by scientific work is important in the sense of "worth being known." (1946: 143)

Two conclusions follow from these accounts. First, Weber believes that the value of scientific research is a culturally derived value that is not necessarily universal. Science is a product of culture; our belief in the value of scientific knowledge is likewise cultural. Weber brings in his argument that no science is presuppositionless to buttress this position: "No science is absolutely free of presuppositions, and no science can prove its fundamental value to the man who rejects these presuppositions" (1946: 153). Second, Weber claims a quasi-universal status for logic. He declares that "even a Chinese" would have to acknowledge the correctness of a scientific proof and/or logical analysis. But at the same time he seems to be conceding that logic, too, is a cultural presupposition, although a very fundamental one, one of the "general foundations of our orientation in the world." What this comes to is something similar to Wittgenstein's understanding of "general facts of nature." Certain beliefs are so foundational that we cannot imagine a world in which they are not operative. For Weber, logic occupies this position. Although the rigor of his analysis forces him to acknowledge that logic is a cultural product, he accords it a special place in our cultural framework because it is so foundational to our culture's view of the world. These two points come together in Weber's assertion: "For scientific truth is precisely what is *valid* for all who *seek* the truth" (1949: 84). The unprovable value presupposition of science is that scientific truth is a valuable goal. This presupposition, like all values, cannot be established scientifically. But if it is embraced, then one, and only one, path will lead us to that goal: logical analysis.

Weber is usually categorized as an adherent of the fact/value dichotomy that defined the positivist philosophy of his day. Two elements of his theory justify this categorization: his well-known assertion that values stand in irreconcilable conflict with each other and that scientific analysis cannot prove the validity of a particular value position and his search for "objective" facts. This characterization, however, ignores the complexity and ambiguity of Weber's approach. Weber's position is in many respects closer to the postmodern view that opposites inhabit each other than to the modernist definition of objectivity. The deconstruction of the fact/value dichotomy and, with it, the concept of objectivity is implicit in the definitions that Weber advances. Weber's definition of the factual sphere, the realm of objectivity, is barely recognizable as "objective" in the modernist sense. The conceptual tool of his social science, the ideal type, is permeated by values; Weber even uses the word "subjective" to describe the method by which ideal types are selected. Furthermore, he defines the basis of his definition of objectivity: the logical method by which concepts are analyzed as a cultural presupposition rather than a universal truth. His is an objectivity defined not by brute facts but by cultural values.

Weber's position seems more compatible with positivism when it comes to his definition of the subjectivity of the value realm. But ambiguities arise here as well. He argues that the realm of values is a realm of irreconcilable conflict: "'Scientific' pleading is meaningless in principle because the various value spheres of the world stand in irreconcilable conflict with each other" (1946: 147). Science cannot tell us which values are "correct." But science, Weber asserts, can be very useful in clarifying the meaning and implications of value positions. Weber lays out an impressive list of the possibilities of the "scientific" analysis of values. This scientific analysis, he argues, can significantly clarify value positions, revealing their logical consistency and practical results (1949: 20–1).[9] Finally, Weber "resolves" the fact/value dichotomy by taking a moral stance: to take a value position we must *choose* a position as our own. "The ultimately possible attitudes toward life are irreconcilable and hence their struggle can never be brought to a final conclusion. Thus it is necessary to make a decisive choice" (1946: 152). Weber asserts that we must take *personal* responsibility for our value choices precisely because they can have no other ground.[10]

Weber's approach to the relationship between facts and values is informed not only by his belief in the nature and possibilities of scientific analysis but also by his understanding of the world in which he lived. What he called the "disenchantment" of the world permeated every aspect of life; it is our inescapable fate, the cross we must bear. "The fate of an epoch which has eaten of the tree of knowledge is that it must know that we cannot learn the *meaning* of the world from the results of its analysis, be it ever so perfect; it must rather be in a position to create this meaning" (1949: 57). Scientific knowledge is both a blessing and a curse. It gives us the certainty of empirically justifiable truth. But it also strips the world of meaning because it reveals the impossibility of proving any ultimate values. This situation creates a particular moral imperative for the scientist. The scientist, understanding both the blessing and the curse of science, must take a moral stance while at the same time understanding the ungroundedness of that stance. For Weber, this is an understanding not available to all of us, and thus places unique moral demands on the scientist.

Weber's thought is both interesting and useful for my purposes, because it moves beyond the dichotomies that define modernist thought. Some aspects of his thought are thoroughly modernist, yet others move in a distinctly postmodern direction.[11] Weber is a very honest writer. In his effort to thoroughly understand what social scientists do and where their concepts originate, he confronts all the hard questions. And his conclusions do not fit neatly into modernist epistemology. He describes partial and "subjective" concepts that are defined as "objective" because they are rooted in a culturally specific definition of logic. Although Weber defines logic and the belief in the value of scientific truth as fundamental to our way of life, this view is a far cry from the modernist concept of objective science. Weber's ideal-typical methodology has been compared to a "mosaic," a set of partial views of social reality that constructs the totality one piece at a time. This is accurate, but must include the proviso that Weber, like the postmoderns, denies the possibility of grasping the totality entirely.[12]

In describing the context of Weber's life, his wife, Marianne, noted that those, like Weber, who "had abandoned the old gods without turning to socialism or the aristocracy of artistry (Nietzschism) felt that they were in 'freedom's empty space'" (M. Weber 1988: 319). Weber's belief that the world is "disenchanted," that it lacks intrinsic meaning, is, for him, both a cause for despair and a challenge. At the end of "Science as a vocation," Weber concludes that each of us must find and obey the demon who holds the fibers of his very life (1946: 156). Weber's demon is living in a world without absolute values. It is hard not to come to the conclusion that Weber would have preferred to live in a world of certain and provable values. But Weber is a pragmatist. Since he does not live in such a world, he concludes that the world in which he does live presents him with a moral imperative: value choice. Since the world lacks meaning, it is incumbent on each person to bestow it with meaning through an act of individual value choice. We must then take responsibility for the values we have chosen.

In *States of Injury* Wendy Brown argues that feminists fear a postmodern politics because they want Truth, not politics as a terrain of struggle, certainty not instability (1995: 37). The same holds true for feminist methodology. Feminists want to justify the truth of their claims about the status of women in society. When they claim that women are oppressed, that they occupy an inferior role in society, they want to substantiate these claims as true. Such substantiation has become difficult in a world in which the epistemological certainties of modernity are crumbling. This is further complicated by the fact that the feminist movement has been one of the major forces in modernity's deconstruction. Yet feminists are reluctant to abandon truth entirely – to assert, with Trebilcot, only subjective truths. It is my contention that Weber provides a way of talking about truth without appealing to modernist certainties. He defines a social science that makes justifiable truth claims without denying the partiality and value-relatedness of that science and the concepts it employs.

Feminist ideal types

In his attempt to justify his tortured examination of social-scientific methodology and, particularly, the ideal type, Weber argues that he is not defining a new method but, rather, describing what social scientists actually do (1949: 43, 94). I am going to borrow this as a justification for my exploration of feminist ideal types. What feminists are doing is path breaking and exciting. But the heated disputes over a feminist methodology that have erupted indicate that there is little unanimity in the feminist community about what it is that we are doing. I want to contribute to this discussion, first, by explaining in some epistemological detail what feminist social scientists are doing when they explain social reality. My second goal is to offer a justification for that activity that does not rely either on modernist concepts of absolute truth, universality, and the separation of facts and values or on the claim to exactly reproduce social reality.

Weber fashioned his concept of the ideal type in response to two, polarized approaches to the social sciences in his day: that of the subjectivists who denied all abstraction and generalization and that of the advocates of a nomothetic social science who wanted to define universal laws of social reality. It is significant that these two positions are represented in contemporary feminist discussions and, as in the *Methodenstreit* of Weber's day, form the two poles of those discussions. Like the subjectivists, some contemporary feminists argue that we must eschew concepts in feminist methodology, that we must anchor our analyses in the "truth" of "women's lives," "women's reality," or "women's experience." They assert that any abstraction from women's lived reality is illegitimate and a concession to the distortions of masculinist social science.[13] At the other extreme are feminist theorists who, like the advocates of nomothetic social science in Weber's day, argue that we must search for the universals of the human condition to ground our empirical and normative research. I have discussed several varieties of this argument. Some feminist standpoint theorists argue that we must retain a notion of the "truth" of the social totality. Some feminist political theorists have argued that we must retain at least a quasi-universalistic conception of human needs to ground feminist theory.

Weber's analysis of the ideal type reveals the epistemological fallacies implicit in each of these positions. The ideal type counters the modern-day subjectivists by emphasizing that the object of the social scientist's investigation, the range from which she chooses her topic, is the set of meanings constituted by social actors. This effectively dispels the notion that we can and must ground feminist analysis in the pre-discursive reality of women's lives. Weber's concept emphasizes that this reality is already constituted by social actors, in this case women. His analysis further reveals that when the social analyst selects an aspect of that discursively constituted reality to study, she must create a concept in order to do so; the feminist analyst must create the concept "women's experience" in order to study that aspect of social reality. Against the modern-day universalists, Weber's theory is equally effective. Weber's theory does more than concede that all concepts are partial and perspectival; it explains precisely why this is the case and why no total view of social reality is either possible or desirable. His argument rests on the assertion that what we want to explain and understand as social scientists is unique social phenomena, not the constitution of global totalities. Although it is possible to define extremely broad commonalities of human life (Peter Winch [1972] suggests birth, death, and sexuality) these generalities will not produce the kind of analyses the social scientist requires. More can be gained by arguing against specific manifestations of need deprivation than by constructing a list of universal human needs.

Weber argues that the formation of the ideal type involves two distinct stages of conceptualization. In the first stage the researcher surveys the range of social actors' concepts, the concepts that constitute social reality, in the second she chooses a particular subset of these concepts according to her interest. In the foregoing I argued that there is a third stage in this process: the employment of the conceptual apparatus and methodological rules of the social scientist's discipline. If we apply this theory to feminist research, some interesting conclusions follow. As feminists began to enter the social sciences, they discovered that the concepts of their disciplines – sociology, political science, economics, history, anthropology – did not include concepts with which to analyze the discursively constituted realm of "women's reality." They found, on the contrary, that it was an exclusively masculine reality that was conceptualized and theorized by social-scientific disciplines; women's reality was invisible. In order to overcome this obstacle, feminists have had to do some fancy epistemological footwork. The first step was to create new analytic concepts that make women's reality visible, that allow the conceptualization and examination of every aspect of women's lives. The second step was to convince nonfeminist colleagues that this analysis was a legitimate aspect of their discipline. Feminists had to craft arguments that their discipline should include the conceptualization and examination of "women's reality." These arguments, although in effect transforming the boundaries of these disciplines, had to intersect with the discourse of the discipline in order to be persuasive to nonfeminist colleagues.

An alternative strategy, obviously, would be to create a new discipline with no connection to the existing social sciences, a feminist science designed to examine this newly conceptualized aspect of social reality. Two factors argue against this strategy. First, although expanding the conceptual boundaries of the social sciences to include "women's experience" entails a radical transformation of those disciplines, it is not an unprecedented move. Weber makes this point persuasively in his discussion of ideal types. In defending the changing concepts of the social sciences vis-à-vis the natural sciences, he argues that, far from indicating the adolescence of these disciplines, "eternal youth" is granted to the social sciences. In a passage that presages Foucault's argument in *The Order of Things* Weber asserts:

It is not the *actual* interconnection of "things," but the *conceptual* connection of *problems* that define the scope of the various sciences. A new "science" emerges where new problems are pursued by new methods and truths are thereby discovered which open up significant new points of view. (1949: 68)

The second argument, which I develop in the concluding chapter, is that casting its arguments in terms acceptable to the hegemonic discourse of masculinist social science is the most effective strategy for feminism. The logic that defines "good science" in these disciplines is, as Weber argued, rooted in the "general foundations of our orientation in the world." Casting arguments outside this logic will succeed only in silencing women's voice. Creating new concepts within the existing disciplines, acting as the outsider within, however, is most likely to alter the discourse of those disciplines.

The epistemological position of the feminist social scientist as I see it, then, is this. She, like every member of her society, conceptualizes the world according to the concepts of the culture/language that she inhabits. This includes, in her case, her reality in a specifically women's realm. Entering one of the social sciences, however, she discovers that the world she knows as a woman is invisible to this science; no concepts are available to grasp and analyze it. This is the "bifurcated consciousness" that feminist social scientists have discussed. This situation forces the feminist social scientist to create new concepts that can analyze "women's reality." But these concepts and the methods she uses to analyze them are not wholly divorced from her discipline. They stretch the boundaries of the discipline while remaining inside it. Finally, the arguments which the feminist social scientist uses to justify her new concepts are ones that make sense to her nonfeminist colleagues; they transform the discipline from within.

There are numerous examples I could use to illustrate this epistemological story. Perhaps the most obvious is women's history. Prior to the women's movement, the discipline of history had defined "historical facts" as, with few exceptions, the activities of elite men in a narrowly defined political arena. The activities of women (and those of men outside the political realm) were only rarely conceptualized; they did not qualify as "historical facts" and thus were excluded from the discipline. When feminist historians began to look at women's lives in history, and other social historians began to look at the lives of African-Americans or working-class white men, the concepts they developed to examine those lives transformed the discipline of history. The boundaries of the discipline were stretched to include a previously unconceptualized reality. It is significant, furthermore, that in bringing a new aspect of social reality into the discipline of history, feminist and social historians also developed new historical methods. Methods are linked to theories and the facts they create. The traditional methods of history were inappropriate for the examination of women's history. These methods focused on sources such as congressional records, politicians' memoirs, legal enactments; women were not present in these sources. The new methods of "social history" had to be created in order to analyze a new category of facts. Feminist and social historians began to look at new sources: oral histories, diaries, census records, material culture, even fiction.

Two conclusions follow from this example. First, the discipline of history has been redefined. "Social history" and "women's history" are now established parts of the discipline of history. Perhaps the clearest indication of this change is that what used to be called "history," the study of elite men's political activities, is now called "traditional political history." What "political history" means has itself been redefined. It can now include the study of slave rebellions, women's moral reform, and other phenomena outside the realm of the strictly "political" sphere. Second, the arguments that feminist historians made for the inclusion of women in the historical record were arguments internal to the discipline itself – at the margins, certainly, but nonetheless within. And these arguments were, in the long run, successful.

Another area in which the emergence of feminist ideal types has been both notable and successful is the law. Ideal types are central to the law as it operates in our society. Laws define types of actions and categories of crimes; they are necessarily generalizing, eliding some differences and emphasizing others. Although the use of concepts in the law differs from that in academic disciplines, epistemologically the concepts are very similar. Legal concepts are one-sided accentuations of social reality designed to synthesize the significant elements of a phenomenon. All the elements of "first degree murder" are not found in every case of premeditated murder, but the concept is a synthesis of the significant elements of the phenomenon from the point of view of a legal order. The ideal types of the law, furthermore, have a uniquely powerful influence in our society; they have very real and material effects on all of us encompassed by the legal system. Legal definitions structure society by defining categories of individuals and their hierarchy within the state. Changes in legal ideal types thus have profound societal effects; these hierarchies can be altered significantly.

These factors explain why much feminist effort has been focused on changing legal categories. In some cases, feminists have concentrated on changing the parameters of an existing ideal type. The concept of "rape" is an example of this strategy. Not very long ago "rape" was, in effect, defined in the law as men's sexual access to women who did not belong to them, to whom access was denied. Thus, to effectively prosecute a rape, it had to be shown that the woman had had no prior sexual relations with the rapist (ideally, he would be a stranger) and that she had put up physical resistance. The concept of marital rape made no sense within this definition; marriage was defined as a man's unlimited sexual access to his wife. The same was true of what we now call "date rape." In the past few decades, however, feminists have succeeded in changing the parameters of the ideal type of rape. The concept has shifted from a definition of the man's relationship to the woman (entitlement) to the woman's consent. This shift has had dramatic consequences for women. Rapes are now prosecuted more aggressively and successfully. Categories of rape that were disallowed under the old ideal type are now recognized. The continued use of the terms "marital rape" and "date rape," however, indicates that feminists have not been completely successful in their redefinition of the ideal type. If rape were defined strictly in terms of a woman's consent, these qualifiers would not be necessary. Their persistence reveals that the association between rape and lack of entitlement has not been completely erased.

Another feminist legal tactic has been to create an ideal type where none existed before, thus bringing under the purview of the law activities that had previously been invisible. The concepts of "domestic violence," "battered woman," and "batterer" that emerged in the 1970s are examples of this strategy. The legal effect of these concepts has been to change the parameters of acceptable male violence in intimate personal relationships. The legal heritage on the issue of domestic violence is dismal. Concepts such as the "rule of thumb" defined the parameters of male violence in intimate relationships. Domestic violence legislation has changed this situation profoundly. It has defined a sphere of activity that was previously invisible to the law and labeled it criminal. "Sexual harassment" is another example of this phenomenon. An activity that was legally invisible has, by the creation of an ideal type, been brought under the purview of the law and criminalized.[14]

These examples illustrate Weber's understanding of the process by which ideal types are formed and how the changing definition of existing ideal types or the creation of new ones can alter the structure of society. The raw material for the ideal types that feminists have changed or created is present in our discursively constituted social reality. Social actors possess concepts of the lives and activities of women as well as the varieties of violence against women. What was missing was the conceptualization of these activities by social analysts, either academic or legal. When feminist historians conceptualized and analyzed the activities of women, they brought this sphere of social reality into their discipline, thereby changing it significantly. When feminist lawyers succeeded in changing the definition of rape and creating legal categories of violence against women, they brought an aspect of social reality that had been invisible to the law to the attention of the legal community. As a result, what had been invisible was made visible and defined as "real."

There is another aspect of feminist social-scientific analysis that is equally significant: exploring new dimensions of the ideal types that are central to both the social sciences and the social institutions they study. The epistemology of these analyses is different: it involves the examination of existing concepts rather than the creation of new ones. But this analysis is significant in that, like the creation of new ideal types, it illuminates a hitherto invisible aspect of social reality. The feminist exploration of the assumptions embedded in the ideal types that structure our social institutions has, as much as the creation of new ideal types, contributed to the feminist transformation of the social sciences. It is significant, furthermore, that what is perhaps Weber's most famous ideal-typical analysis, *The Protestant Ethic and the Spirit of Capitalism*, employs this type of analysis.

A good example of feminist analysis of this type that elaborates on a particularly Weberian theme is Kathy Ferguson's *The Feminist Case Against Bureaucracy* (1984). In her book Ferguson reveals the assumptions about human beings embedded in the ideal type of bureaucracy, resisting and contesting those assumptions. In a complex, multilayered analysis, Ferguson reveals how the concept of domination inherent in bureaucratic organization impinges on the lives of women. Her principal conclusion is that domination is feminized: to be dominated means to be feminine. Thus Ferguson argues that "women are not powerless because they are feminine; rather they are feminine because they are powerless" (1984: 95). This leads her to a yet more radical conclusion: the futility of "liberating" women to take an equal place in bureaucratic institutions. If domination is coded masculine, being dominated feminine, then women can only dominate by becoming men, by renouncing their femininity and imposing domination/femininity on others (1984: 122).

Although the structure of Ferguson's analysis differs from that of feminists who create new ideal types, it has much the same effect. Bureaucracies are ubiquitous; they are, as Weber himself so clearly argued, central to modern life. Ferguson's analysis reveals a dimension of bureaucratic organization that Weber and other theorists of bureaucracy ignored: its gender coding. She looks at Weber's ideal type of bureaucracy from the perspective of the feminist interest in gender and reveals the masculine character of its domination. In the course of her analysis, Ferguson also wants to suggest a new discourse in which bureaucratic dominance would be replaced. But the parameters of this discourse remain vague. The real impact of her work is to reveal the gender implications of a phenomenon central to our social organization.

Most social and political theorists, both feminist and nonfeminist, would agree that the ideal type that forms the central core of modern social and political theory, as well as the social sciences, is that of the rational, autonomous individual. This ideal type informs all the major actors in the drama of modernity: the citizen, the moral agent, the rational thinker, the scientist. Deconstructing this ideal type and revealing its inherently gendered character has been one of the significant achievements of feminist social and political theory. There are many notable texts in this tradition. Susan Moller Okin's *Women in Western Political Thought* (1979), Jean Bethke Elshtain's *Public Man, Private Woman* (1981), Susan Bordo's *The Flight to Objectivity* (1987), and Carole Pateman's *The Sexual Contract* (1988) are some of the most influential. Although any of these texts could illustrate my point, Pateman's discussion offers a particularly clear example of the epistemological implications of this analysis. Pateman focuses on what she calls the "origin story" of the social contract, the story that provides the justification for contemporary liberal democracies. She argues convincingly that the individual who signs the social contract in Locke's story is necessarily defined as a husband and a father. It is essential to Locke's definition of the individual citizen that he possess wife, children, and property; without all these attributes he cannot be admitted to free citizenship. Pateman then goes on to argue that this definition precludes the possibility of political equality for women. Since women cannot possess the necessary attributes of citizenship, they can never attain true equality. The concept that forms the foundation of liberal democracy is necessarily gendered masculine. Full political equality for women is not possible within the reality created by this ideal type.

In her book Pateman suggests an alternative ideal type: the embodied citizen. She argues that women can only be politically equal if their embodiment *as women* becomes a part of the definition of citizenship: "To take embodied identity seriously demands the abandonment of the masculine, unitary individual to open up space for two figures: one masculine, one feminine" (1988: 224). But this concept is given only a vague outline in Pateman's book. It remains an ideal to be attained, rather than a description of an existing phenomenon. Despite this, I think that the analysis of Pateman and other feminists who have deconstructed the ideal types of our fundamental social and political institutions can profitably be understood in terms of Weber's methodology. We cannot conceptualize and create a new ideal type of citizenship until we understand the full implications of the one we have. We cannot conceptualize the embodied citizen that Pateman envisions until we understand that our concept excludes her. Weber argued that new sciences are created by looking at new problems from a new perspective. Feminists in this tradition have outlined the first step in this process: taking a new perspective on a problem that did not exist in traditional political theory – gendered citizenship. The next step, which has not yet been accomplished, is to create new concepts.[15]

Conclusion

In the foregoing I have surveyed a range of approaches to feminist method. I have argued against the two extremes in the debate over feminist method: those who eschew any universal concepts and generalizations and those who argue for a necessary grounding in universal concepts. I have, instead, attempted to define a kind of middle ground. Like Nancy Fraser, I argue that we need "frameworks that are sensitive to specificity, but that nevertheless permit us to grasp very large objects of inquiry" (1995: 159). I have turned to Weber because his concept of the ideal type provides a sophisticated epistemological justification for just such a broad range of concepts. It has been my contention that feminists require a new epistemological understanding to justify the concepts they employ. The advocates of difference and diversity must be answered, but so must the critics of "difference without end." I think that Weber's theory can provide this needed justification.

A Weberian justification of feminist social analysis rests on three principle arguments. First, the concepts that feminists employ are unavowedly political and value-laden. Weber offers a persuasive argument for the necessarily value-laden character of all social-scientific concepts. He reveals the futility of defining objectivity as value-neutrality. On his account, all social-scientific concepts are "subjective" in the sense of value-laden. Thus feminist concepts are not unique in this respect. They are not "biased" in contrast to the "objective" concepts of masculinist social science, because all concepts are biased. One of the strengths of feminist social analysis, furthermore, has been to expose the bias of the allegedly neutral concepts of masculinist social science.

Second, feminist concepts are partial concepts; they do not reveal the truth of social reality in its totality, because no concepts are able to do this. Again, in this respect feminist concepts do not differ from other social-scientific concepts. But there is a sense in which the partiality of feminist concepts has served a unique purpose. The creation of feminist ideal types has revealed the falsity of the claim to universality made for the general concepts of masculinist social science. By revealing hitherto invisible aspects of social reality, feminists' concepts expose the partiality of masculinist "general" concepts.

Third, feminist concepts are justified on the basis of a single overriding criterion: does the concept help us *understand* social reality? This is the most significant aspect of Weber's perspective. Modernist epistemology justifies general concepts on the basis of their truth function. If a concept corresponds to reality and no counterexamples exist, then it is "true." Specific concepts, on the other hand, are justified in a negative sense: they are right because they do not abstract from the concreteness of brute social reality. In recent feminist discussions this has meant that the concept does not elide differences that exist in that reality. Weber reveals the flaws in both these justifications. We cannot grasp social reality in its totality; thus "getting it right" cannot be our criterion of which concepts to use. We do not disprove an ideal type, Weber asserts, by finding a counter example, but, rather, by showing that it fails to illuminate social reality. Abstraction from concrete reality, furthermore, is not an illegitimate method employed by social analysis that distorts social reality. Rather, it is a necessary part of all discursive activity. Describing any experience, even the most simple, always involves concepts and thus is culturally coded. We need to justify the concepts we use, but their abstraction from concrete reality does not, in itself, disqualify them.

Applying Weber's criterion to both general and specific feminist concepts has fruitful consequences. General feminist concepts elide differences among women; they purport to offer truths about all women. If we judge these concepts on the basis of whether counterinstances exist, they fail; they do not, in fact, offer truths about all women. But if we judge them according to whether they illuminate social reality, many of them pass muster. Theories by "gender theorists" such as Gilligan and Chodorow have fostered our understanding of the constitution of women's oppression and how it can be eradicated. They have provided valuable insights into the broad parameters of women's situation; they have changed the landscape of social and political analysis and theory.[16]

Specific feminist concepts are useful in a different sense. As critics such as Susan Bordo have pointed out, analyses that foster difference without differentiation will do little to improve women's situation. But it is also the case that feminism's recent emphasis on differences has enriched our understanding of women's situation. The elision of differences that characterized the gender theories of the 1980s had disadvantages as well as advantages. The race, class, ethnic, and other differences among women were obscured; the privileging of white middle-class Anglo-American women was invisible. The focus on differences has been a positive and necessary corrective to these theories. But we can go too far in this direction. Some analyses of differences are useful, in that they foster our understanding of women's diverse situations; some are not. Some differences are more pervasive than others. Some structure the parameters of our lives; others are trivial. Some are imposed on us to our detriment; others are chosen. We need to constantly negotiate these differences, using the criterion of understanding to make what are admittedly difficult decisions regarding the utility of concepts.

It should be obvious at this point that the criterion I (following Weber) am proposing raises difficult questions. How can I convince other feminists that the analysis I propose does, in fact, illuminate social reality? Or serve the goal of relieving the oppression of women? There are no easy answers to these questions. The modernist answer – that the analysis reveals the Truth of social reality – is no longer available to us. What are available to us are arguments. I can use arguments to convince other feminists that my feminist concepts are useful. The fact that we share the same goal – improving the material situation of women – should give us some common ground. The ongoing disputes within feminism, however, reveal that agreement is not a foregone conclusion.

Convincing nonfeminists is even trickier. I argued above that most feminist social analysts employ arguments that intersect with the methodological norms of their discipline. They use the methods of history, political science, sociology, or economics to argue for the validity of their theories and concepts. When these arguments have been successful, the result has been the reshaping of those disciplines. But, ultimately, feminist arguments will not only reshape but transform these disciplines. Epistemologically, feminist concepts challenge the modernist epistemology of mainstream social science. Feminist concepts reveal that all concepts are partial, political, and chosen according to the interests of the investigator. This is not an argument that many contemporary social scientists will accept. The modernist presumption that concepts correspond to social reality is still prevalent in many social sciences. In short, feminist arguments will be difficult to make because, ultimately, they entail a radical redefinition of social science.

The solution to the epistemological and methodological problems faced by contemporary feminism that I am offering cannot be reduced to a neat formula. What it comes down to is that feminists must construct arguments that are both convincing in the terms of the hegemonic discourse and at the same time transform that discourse. What this solution does not entail, however, is clear: the appeal to a metanarrative of "Truth." We may yearn for a world in which truth claims can be justified by reference to a metanarrative, but we no longer live in such a world, if we ever did. The metanarrative that held sway for so long rests on a false claim to universality; any metanarrative that might replace it will be similarly partial. Like it or not, we *do* live in a world in which many voices vie for ascendancy. Our question should be not how we can reestablish a metanarrative more to our liking, but how we can make our voice heard among the cacophony of voices. Specifically, how can we construct arguments that feminist ideal types are valid because conceptualizing the world through these concepts would yield a better world?

Despite this rejection of the modernist metanarrative, however, my solution does not conform to many postmodern formulations. For many postmoderns the question of how to formulate a new methodology for feminist social science is both irrelevant and dangerous. They see no need to formulate a methodological position and define the impulse to do so as harking back to the oppressive nature of modernist thought. Against this I am arguing that unless we define a new methodological approach, we will lose the constitutive aspect of feminist analysis: social critique.

I take up the epistemological details of this question in the last chapter. My emphasis here is methodological rather than epistemological. It is my argument that the methodology of the ideal type sketched above offers an understanding of how feminist research operates in the contemporary theoretical and political climate. Feminist ideal types are political and engaged. They carve up the social world differently from the ideal types of masculinist theory. In defense of these ideal types, we can do nothing but argue that our perspective reveals oppressions that society should work to eradicate. By employing ideal types that "see" the world differently, feminists undermine the structures that constitute that world and work to transform it.[17]

4

The Epistemology of Moral Voice: Displacing Hegemony in Moral/Legal Discourse

The methodological problems raised by an exploration of the differences among women are complex. Particularly in the social sciences, they require a new justification for analytic concepts and a new means of justifying the truth claims made by feminist analysts. The methodological problems facing feminism, however, are derivative of another even more difficult problem: articulating a new epistemology of differences. This problem involves no less a task than redefining the epistemology that has dominated the Western tradition, particularly since the advent of modernity. The hegemonic discourse of Western epistemology is unitary: Truth is defined as singular and universal; it can be attained by only one path. As a consequence, this epistemology defines difference as inferiority. Any deviation from the one Truth, the one path to knowledge, is necessarily inferior simply because it is a difference, a deviation.

This epistemology of difference permeates every aspect of Western thought, creating hierarchies that differentiate the superior from the inferior. It has had a particularly profound effect on understandings of the relation between men and women. Women deviate from the standard defined by men and thus are necessarily inferior. The crux of this difference has been defined in terms of rationality. Women have been labeled inferior because they are incapable of achieving the Truth that is accessible to the ideally rational man. It is significant that both the first and the second strategies of contemporary feminism conform to this epistemology of difference. The first strategy's erasure of difference fostered the argument that women are capable of attaining Truth because, like men, they can achieve rationality. Advocates of the second strategy attempted to reverse this equation. Emphasizing the difference between men and women, they claimed that women's essential nature is superior to that of men, that it is men who are inferior. But they did not challenge the epistemology that requires a single true standard from which deviations are defined as inferior.

The third strategy, by contrast, requires a radically different epistemology, an epistemology that eschews unitary truth and articulates, instead, multiple paths to truth. To pursue the third strategy, feminists must develop an epistemology that treats differences differently: not as inferior deviations from the one true standard, but as legitimate expressions of the varieties of human life and experience. They must do so, furthermore, with a clear understanding of the nature and extent of the hegemonic discourse they oppose. Specifically, feminists must develop strategies that will displace this hegemony and open up paths to a new epistemology. In the next two chapters I approach this task by looking at moral discourse and the discourse of epistemology. My goal is to define strategies that will accomplish the feminist goal of redefining what constitutes a true statement.

Different moral voices

Although the concept of "woman" has become suspect in many aspects of feminism, this exclusion has not applied to feminist moral theory. Discussions in feminist moral theory are, with a few exceptions, dominated by the problematic of the second strategy; analyses of the differences between the moral voices of men and women are its central preoccupation. Several factors account for this situation. Most important is the far-reaching influence of Carol Gilligan's *In a Different Voice* (1982). Gilligan's work placed the moral difference between men and women at the center of feminist discussions. Her discussion of women's moral voice resonated strongly with many women; defining the "care" voice thus set the parameters for the discussion of women and morality. The result has been a polarized discussion involving an extensive analysis of the relationship between the voices of justice and care. Almost missing from this discussion, however, has been an analysis of the variety of moral voices among women or the ways in which the gendered constitution of morality varies according to the influence of other social factors. Although critics of Gilligan have argued that her discussion is limited to white, middle-class women (Stack 1990), the varieties of women's moral voices has not become a central feature of the discussion of women's different voice.[1]

A second factor is the tradition of moral discourse as it has evolved in Western thought. Although the twentieth century has seen numerous attempts to deconstruct modernist epistemology, to define multiple paths to truth, a parallel effort in moral discourse has been decidedly lacking. Deconstructing the unitary epistemology of Western thought is, admittedly, a challenging task. But there is a sense in which such an endeavor is academic, the concern of philosophers removed from the "real world." Deconstructing the hegemonic unitary conception of moral truth, however, is a different order of things. Moral discourse has real-life applications; the threat of moral anarchy constrains discussions of multiple moral voices. Despite contemporary discussions of "moral relativism,"[2] most moral philosophers feel compelled to come up with some definitive answer to the question "What is moral?" It is significant that feminist moral theory has also been influenced by these constraints. Discussions of the different moral voice of women have revolved around the replacement of the justice voice by the feminine voice of care. Epistemologically, this alternative remains within the parameters of the hegemonic moral tradition: one true, universal definition of morality is replaced by another; the epistemology of one true moral voice is unaltered. Although some feminists (significantly, Gilligan herself) have argued that there are two equally valid moral voices, the epistemological significance of this argument is rarely explored. The possibility of more than two moral voices, furthermore, almost never arises.

It is not difficult to cite examples of this phenomenon. A symposium on care and justice was held at the 1994 American Political Science Association convention and was published in a subsequent volume of *Hypatia*. In this symposium two of the best-known "care" theorists, Joan Tronto and Virginia Held, explored the question of the best or most comprehensive framework for moral, political, and legal questions. Held argued that care is the "most basic" moral value, the wider moral framework into which justice should be fitted (1995: 131). Tronto took a different approach but, like Held, concluded that the care approach is the "best" framework for moral and political judgments (1995: 141).

Discussions of the feminine moral voice of care have been a fruitful development in feminist thought. They begin the necessary task of deconstructing the hegemony of the justice voice. But attempting to displace this hegemony by proclaiming the superiority of the care voice is not an effective strategy for feminist moral theory. By arguing that the moral voice of care is superior to that of justice – that is, that it provides the better and more comprehensive moral framework – feminist discussions perpetuate the hegemonic moral and epistemological assumptions of the Western tradition. What is required, however, is an epistemological alternative that provides an understanding of multiple moral voices, that can incorporate differences nonhierarchically.

Articulating this alternative must begin with an approach to the epistemology of the care voice that does not involve defining a hierarchy of care and justice. Gilligan's argument rests on the assertion that gender is constitutive in the formation of moral voice; her approach suggests that morality is particular, contextual, and socially constructed. This understanding of morality offers a sharp contrast to the impartial, abstract paradigm that defines the justice voice. The hegemonic discourse of the justice voice defines the moral realm as disembodied, transcending all social and cultural influences, including gender. Indeed, it assumes that the removal of social and cultural influences is a necessary prerequisite to the definition of moral principles. Gilligan counters this not just by suggesting that the feminine voice of care is constructed, but by defining moral voice *per se* as constructed. In her formulation, both the care *and* the justice voice are constructed in conjunction with the formation of the gendered self. Thus, in an epistemological sense, Gilligan is not integrating another moral voice into existing moral discourse but redefining the moral realm itself.

Gilligan does not develop the epistemological implications of her position. But the significance of her position is reinforced by the fact that, despite her emphasis on the care voice, she refuses to privilege the care voice over the justice voice. Although Gilligan's work has spawned a literature whose central presupposition is the superiority of the care voice, Gilligan herself does not take this position. She consistently asserts that the two moral voices are equally valid, not that the voice of care is superior. She frequently reiterates her claim that her goal is to replace a unitary moral discourse with a discourse of nonhierarchical duality. Although she does not explicitly acknowledge it, however, Gilligan's refusal to privilege one voice offers a clear contrast to the hegemonic moral discourse, a discourse predicated on the existence of a single, universal standard of moral judgment. This discourse cannot tolerate the existence of two, much less many, moral voices or standards. Once more, Gilligan is not integrating but redefining morality.

Gilligan's insistence on both the social constitution and the equality of the two moral voices suggests an alternative moral epistemology that places difference at its center. Gilligan focuses on the constitutive force of gender in the formation of moral voice, arguing for the validity of the different voice of women. But once the different construction of moral voice is posited, two questions immediately arise. First, if one social influence, gender, is constitutive in the formation of moral voice, why not others as well? Once we argue for the constitutive role of gender, it seems obvious that other social factors – class, race, ethnicity – will also be constitutive of moral voice. Second, if gender is constitutive of moral voice, is it not the case that gender is coded differently according to a variety of social factors? There is not one gender coding, but many; the gender coding that a white, middle-class woman will encounter will be quite different from that of an African-American woman on welfare.[3]

In chapter 2 I argued that feminist standpoint theory, by positing the social construction of knowledge, pointed beyond the second strategy's emphasis on difference to the third strategy of differences. A similar argument applies to Gilligan's approach. Once she deconstructs the disembodied rationality of the justice voice and jettisons a single, universal standard, the road to a moral epistemology of differences is open. Gilligan focuses on the difference that gender makes in the moral realm. But her approach suggests that more differences than those between men and women are epistemologically significant in the construction of moral voice.

Contemplating a moral epistemology of multiple moral voices, however, raises disturbing questions. If we embrace such an epistemology and hence reject a universal standard, how would we choose among moral voices? How could we declare anything to be "right"? How could a legal system function? In the following I begin to address these questions.[4] Two related tasks are primary. The first is to define an alternative moral epistemology of multiple moral voices and to explore how the hegemony of the universal, abstract moral paradigm can be displaced by such an epistemology. In order to address this question, I focus on legal discourse, the embodiment of the justice voice in the Western tradition. The second task is to determine how to choose among moral voices, how to decide which moral voice is appropriate in a particular moral context. Without offering a detailed argument, I conclude by sketching the outline of an answer to this question.

I noted above that the twentieth century has seen several attempts to define multiple paths to truth, while a parallel effort to define multiple paths to moral truth has been lacking. This statement needs qualification. There have been numerous attempts to define what contemporary moral theorists call "moral relativism." The problem with these discussions from a feminist perspective, however, is that they do not deal with the issues that a feminist critique requires. In their discussions of approaches to morality, most theorists of moral relativism ignore the fact that must be the starting point of the feminist critique: the hegemony of the justice voice and the devaluation of alternative and, especially, "feminine" approaches to morality. They also ignore questions of power and subjectivity that must be central features of a feminist moral theory. They thus offer little help in the task of constructing a feminist alternative.[5]

But there is another source that can offer guidance: contemporary epistemological theories. Because of their common philosophical roots, the arguments that contemporary epistemologists have constructed against modernist epistemology can be applied to modernist moral theory as well. I rely on two of these arguments here. The first is that of Hans-Georg Gadamer. In *Truth and Method* (1975) Gadamer attacks the notion that truth is defined in singular terms, arguing instead that there is more than one path to truth. Specifically, he asserts that the exclusive association between truth and the scientific/ logical method is misguided. Against this unitary epistemology he proposes a hermeneutic epistemology of location and context. Our experience of truth, he asserts, is not limited to the abstract, universalizing method defined by logic and the natural sciences; that truth, he asserts, is the exception rather than the rule.

What might be called Gadamer's deconstruction of modernist epistemology has two principal thrusts. First, he suggests an alternative, hermeneutic epistemology that posits many paths to truth. Second, he turns the modernist argument on its head by suggesting that the abstract, universalizing method, far from constituting the single paradigm of all truth, is, instead, an exception, even an aberration. Our paradigmatic experience of truth, on Gadamer's account, is contextual and particular. This point is encapsulated in his concept of "prejudice," the pre-judgments that he defines as making all understanding possible. His hermeneutic approach presupposes that we always understand from within a context, a particular location that defines meaning for us. From Gadamer's perspective, then, the "truth" defined by the method of the natural sciences and logic is an unusual and infrequent occurrence – not a paradigm, but an irregularity.[6]

There are striking parallels between Gilligan's approach to moral theory and Gadamer's definition of truth. Implicit in Gilligan's work are assumptions that transform moral epistemology in the same way as Gadamer's work transforms epistemology. At the core of Gilligan's argument is her contention that morality is always contextual, that the moral voices of situated subjects are constituted by their experiences. Like Gadamer, Gilligan argues that the abstract, universalizing model is an aberration rather than the typical case. The striving for abstraction that characterizes the justice voice, the attempt to formulate moral arguments that eschew connection and context, she claims, is an "adolescent ideal" (1982: 98). Her contrast between the justice voice and the care voice is rooted in her understanding of how the different gendered experiences of girls and boys in our society produce different moral voices. The modernist tradition against which Gilligan is arguing asserts that autonomous, abstract justice – "true morality" – is an essential, universal human trait. Against this, Gilligan argues that *both* moral voices are products of social and discursive forces. She asserts that it is not the case, as women have been told, that women's situatedness prevents them from perceiving moral truth. Rather, her point is that both the autonomy characteristic of men's moral voice and the connectedness characteristic of women's are constituted by their different locations.

Another way of putting this is that the significance of Gilligan's work is that it reveals that modernist moral theory misunderstands the nature of moral truth. Gilligan rejects the modernist presupposition that moral truth is singular and universal, abstract and autonomous. Rather, she asserts, in a Gadamerian spirit, that it is hermeneutic: local and contextual. A Gadamerian reading of Gilligan suggests that her work is not an effort to "get it right" in moral theory, to replace the justice voice with the care voice, but, rather, to introduce an alternative moral epistemology that posits many (or at least two) paths to moral truth. This reading produces an understanding of moral truth that is situated, particular, and, most importantly, multiple.

My second epistemological guide is Stephen Toulmin. Like Gadamer, Toulmin attacks the paradigm that defines a single path to truth. In *The Uses of Argument* he examines the claim that grounds modernist epistemology: "logic is the laws of thought" (1958: 3). In a careful analysis of the structure of various kinds of arguments, he develops the thesis that what he calls the "Court of Reason" can be approached by different paths. His principal point is that although the *force* of an argument is invariant, judging the *strength* of any

particular case is "field-dependent," that is, relative to the appropriate evidence (1958: 38). The target of Toulmin's argument is the
deification of a particular kind of argument, what he calls the "analytic syllogism." The analytic syllogism, like the concept of truth that
Gadamer attacks, is defined by its simplicity and abstraction. Conceding that simplicity has its merits, Toulmin nevertheless argues that
by treating the simplest argument as the paradigm of all truth, "we
may end up thinking that, for some regrettable reason hidden deep in
the nature of things, only our original peculiarly simple arguments
are capable of attaining to the ideal of validity" (1958: 144).

Toulmin echoes Gadamer's argument that this paradigm, far from
defining the typical case, is instead exceptional. The development of
logical theory, Toulmin asserts, began with a special class of arguments: unequivocal, analytic, formally valid arguments with a universal statement as a formal premise. The characteristics of this class
of arguments have been interpreted by logicians as signs of special
merit. But, Toulmin argues, "analytic arguments are a special case,
and we are laying up trouble for ourselves, both in logic and epistemology, if we treat them as anything else" (1958: 145). Toulmin's
goal is to open the "Court of Reason" to arguments that do not
conform to the analytic syllogism and its "timeless truths." This is
importantly different from Gadamer's desire to open the definition of
"truth" to experiences such as art. But Toulmin's conclusion is one
that Gadamer could strongly endorse:

> The superstition that the truth or falsity, validity or justification of all
> our statements and arguments should be entirely independent of the
> circumstances in which they are uttered, may be deeply rooted; but
> away from the timeless conclusions and analytic argument of pure
> mathematics the expectations to which it leads are bound to be dis-
> appointed. The concept of knowledge is not like that, and philo-
> sophers are asking for trouble if they treat it as though it were.
> (1958: 240)

Both Gadamer and Toulmin are, in effect, deconstructing modernist epistemology by arguing against the hegemony of the abstract,
universalizing paradigm that defines truth. They question, rather
than presuppose, the hegemonic status of the modernist paradigm;
they highlight this hegemony and expose its unfounded assertions.
Specifically, they reveal the Achilles' heel of that paradigm: its exceptional character. Although the universal, abstract model of epistemology is hegemonic, it is also, in practice, an exception, an aberration.

These epistemological perspectives have direct parallels in moral epistemology. What Gilligan calls the justice voice in moral discourse is, like the abstract model of truth, hegemonic in Western thought. The justice voice defines what moral truth is; any other definition is ruled out. The work of Gilligan and other feminist theorists of the care voice have revealed the limitations of this definition and begun the task of defining an alternative. They have argued for an understanding of moral truth as local and contextual, rooted in the concrete situations of moral subjects.

But these arguments are just the first step. Defining an alternative moral epistemology in the face of the deep-rootedness of the justice voice is a daunting task. The principal obstacle to this task is the threat of moral anarchy, the fear that unless we define another, singular, true path to morality, we are inviting chaos and disorder. Unless this threat can be successfully negotiated, no alternative moral epistemology can emerge.

Different legal voices

The most concrete embodiment of the hegemony of what Gilligan calls the justice voice is the structure of the legal system in Western democracies. The law concretizes the abstract impartiality of the justice voice in the institution of the rule of law: the impartial judge assessing the facts of a case and applying a universal law. The law also offers a graphic example of Gilligan's analysis of the gendering of the justice voice. One of the principal goals of Western rationalized legal practice is to eradicate the particular in favor of the impartial and universal as much as is humanly possible. Jurors are carefully questioned regarding their connection to the case at hand; they are excused if such a connection exists. They are questioned about their ability to render an "impartial" judgment. Likewise, judges are expected to recuse themselves if they have any connection to a case. Even more significantly, until quite recently, women were assumed to be incapable of the abstraction from particulars necessary to achieve impartiality and thus were excused from jury duty altogether. In short, the law actualizes the gendered division between abstract masculinity and particular femininity.

If feminists want to destabilize this hegemony and begin the process of defining an alternative moral epistemology, then the law presents the greatest challenge to that effort. It seems obvious that if our legal system does not rely on a single, universal standard to legitimize legal judgments, the very fabric of society will be threatened. The ideology of the rule of law provides just such a clear-cut, stable legitimation of moral / legal judgments in our society. At the root of this ideology is a belief borrowed from the justice voice: if we abstract from the particulars of individual cases and our own particular circumstances and apply universal principles, then "truth" will win out. Although even the advocates of this ideology concede that this is only sometimes – its critics would say rarely – the case, it nevertheless exerts a powerful influence on our moral and legal systems. Because of the reality and immediacy of the law, furthermore, it appears to be one area in which contemplating a moral epistemology of multiple moral voices is both ill-conceived and dangerous. It thus provides the clearest test of such an epistemology.

Gadamer and Toulmin described the hegemony of the abstract, universalizing paradigm in epistemology. Max Weber does much the same for the hegemony of a similar paradigm in Western legal discourse: the impartiality model. Weber's examination of the evolution of legal practices in the West is a function of his comprehensive examination of the development of rationalism in the West. In this case Weber wants to find out why the West developed a highly rationalized legal system while other societies did not. In his analysis, Weber ignores issues of gender; for Weber gender is not a significant category of social analysis. Reading Weber across feminist discussions of the masculinization of reason and rationality, however, is revealing. From a feminist perspective, the story Weber is telling is a description of how feminine qualities have been subverted in Western thought and how the masculine definition of rationality has achieved almost undisputed dominance.

Weber's analysis of the character and evolution of Western legal practices has two purposes. First, he wants to pinpoint the unique character of Western law: rationality. Weber defines two senses in which Western law can be described as rational: generalizability – the reduction of reasons relevant in the decision of concrete cases to one or more principles – and systematization – the integration of all legal propositions into a seamless web (1978b: 655–6). In contrast to this, he defines "irrational" lawmaking and law finding as occurring when a "decision is influenced by concrete factors of the particular case as evaluated upon an ethical, emotional, or political basis rather than by general norms" (1978b: 656). It would be difficult to find a clearer statement of the gendering of moral epistemology that has characterized Western thought since Plato. The abstract and universal (masculine) is defined as the ideal and only true form, the particular and concrete (feminine) as its opposite and inferior.

Weber's second task is to explain how this rational legal practice developed in the West. What emerges from his account is, significantly, not the story of an inexorable process of development toward the present rationalized system but, rather, a complex picture of the play of conflicting forces. The rationalizing tendencies which he identifies include Roman law, the canon law of Christendom, the extension of princes' political authority, the demand for rational procedures emanating from groups engaging in rational economic activity, and the development of academic law teaching. Weber waxes particularly eloquent on this last influence. He argues that it was the academization of the law that resulted in the uniquely abstract character of our legal system. The law's removal from concrete cases, he argues, produced "a far-reaching emancipation of legal thinking from the everyday needs of the public" and the "blind desire for logical consistency" (1978b: 789).

But Weber documents opposing forces as well. English common law, German customary law, and the practice of jury trials resisted the formalization of legal practices, preventing the complete rationalization of the law; calls for substantive rather than formal justice could not be silenced completely. For my purposes, the most revealing aspect of Weber's analysis in this respect is his discussion of "Kadi" justice. Weber defines Kadi justice as the adjudication of individual cases by charismatic justice or informal judgments rendered in terms of concrete ethical principles (1978b: 976). Two elements of this definition are significant. First, cases are settled not by reference to a systematic code of laws but by the unique qualities of individual cases. Second, the criteria of justice are substantive, concrete ethical standards, not abstract, universal principles.

Weber's discussion of Kadi justice is far from historically accurate. The operation of Kadi justice in Islamic countries involved the application of divine law as revealed in the Koran; it operated under extreme procedural limitations that allowed no judicial discretion. Weber took elements of this actual institution and, in the spirit of his ideal-typical methodology, developed an ideal type for his own specific purposes: contrasting substantive, particularistic and flexible justice to procedural, rationalized justice. For Weber the ideal type of Kadi justice is not the Islamic judge but the biblical Solomon: the all-wise judge who acts not on the basis of formal laws but according to his perception of the course of justice in each particular case. The point of Weber's ideal type of Kadi justice is that it has the potential to achieve the truest justice of any form of adjudication; unfortunately, it also has the greatest potential for abuse because it includes no safeguards against unscrupulous judges.

Although elements of what Weber calls Kadi justice remain today – English common law, many jury decisions, and justices of the peace – the formalizing tendencies of Western law have been successful in both marginalizing and discrediting this form of justice. Significantly, Weber does not question the normative implications of this trend. He is unequivocal in his judgment that Kadi justice is a throwback to an inferior, primitive stage in the development of legal practices, characterized by kinship groups before the evolution of modern states. "The primitive formalistic irrationality of these older forms of justice," he states, was cast off by the emerging authority of princes and magistrates (1978b: 809).

Both Gadamer and Toulmin argue that, despite the exceptional character of the abstract, universalizing paradigm in epistemology, it has established hegemony as the only path to truth. Weber finds a similar pattern in legal discourse and practice. Much of his analysis involves a description of how various approaches to legal issues vied for dominance and how formal rationality, despite its uniqueness and the infrequency with which it occurred, overcame other approaches and established hegemony. The hegemony of the "blind desire for logical consistency" that Weber documents is the legal manifestation of Gadamer's description of the identification of truth with scientific method and Toulmin's description of the hegemony of the analytic syllogism. The analyses differ in that Weber applauds this development, while Gadamer and Toulmin deplore it. The cases are similar, however, in that the paradigm they describe is at the same time hegemonic and aberrant.

Weber's analysis also parallels aspects of Gilligan's approach. Although they are far from identical, there are significant similarities between what Gilligan and other feminist moral theorists have labeled the care voice and Weber's discussion of Kadi justice. In Weber's ideal type of Kadi justice the judge pays attention to the unique qualities of individual cases and relies on concrete rather than abstract principles. Both these qualities are central to Gilligan's description of the care voice. She defines the care voice in terms of its attention to the particular aspects of concrete moral problems and its rejection of abstract principles. Another similarity lies in Weber's definition of Kadi justice as primitive, irrational, and inferior, a throwback to underdeveloped legal practices. Critics of the care voice have described it as an inferior moral practice lacking in definitive criteria. Weber argues that the rejection of Kadi justice was justified by its lack of definitive criteria; the critics of the care voice make much the same argument. Finally, Weber's documentation of the absence of substantive justice from formalistic legal practice parallels Gilligan's account. Weber states: "Formal justice and the 'freedom' which it guarantees are indeed rejected by all groups ideologically interested in substantive justice. Such groups are better served by Kadi-justice than by the formal type" (1978b: 813). This statement helps explain why feminists and other protest groups have found the legal system inadequate to their goals. It also explains why feminists have theorized the care voice to oppose the formalism of the justice voice. Weber's analysis reveals why it is only by appeal to this voice that feminists and other advocates of social change can attain their goals.

In front of the Supreme Court building in Washington, D.C., stands a statue of a blindfolded woman, whom the sculptor named "Contemplation of Justice." The woman is holding the scales of justice in her hand. Opposite her is a statute of a man, "Guardian of Authority of Law." The statue of the woman is the visual representation of Weber's argument that the paradigm of our legal thought is the impartial, rational observer (portrayed here, interestingly, as a woman, albeit supported by male authority) adjudicating by reference to universally applicable laws; the rule of law, not men. Weber's analysis documents the establishment of this hegemony of the impartial judge in Western legal practice. But although his work is limited to the evolution of legal discourse, it has implications that far exceed this domain. The impartial judge of the rationalistic Western legal tradition is a function of the paradigm that defines the hegemonic discourse of Western moral thought. Gilligan's work demonstrates this very clearly. The justice voice is defined by its abstraction and its reliance on universal principles. The hegemony of this voice, furthermore, is almost unquestioned. Gilligan's analysis documents that, for both men and women, the highest stage of the justice voice is simply what morality *is*. In her discussion of this issue, Judith Sklar puts this point very succinctly: "The value placed on impartiality is, lastly, supreme. The impartial observer is the hero of moral theory, as the impartial judge is the embodiment of justice" (1964: 61–2).

The analyses of the evolution and structure of the ideal type of the impartial observer by Gadamer, Toulmin, Weber, and Gilligan reveal the extent of its hegemony. But they also reveal its vulnerability and hence suggest strategies for displacing that hegemony. In *Truth and Method* Gadamer argues that defining truth as the exclusive product of logic and the scientific method violates our experience of truth; we experience truth in a variety of ways not limited by this paradigm. Gilligan makes much the same kind of argument in her analysis of women's moral voice. She details the structure of women's moral deliberations, deliberations guided by care, connection, and particularity, rather than abstract justice. She then asks us to accept these moral deliberations as a moral discourse equal to that of the justice voice. Another way of putting both these arguments is that if we look at what we actually *do* in the realms of epistemology and morality, we find a variety of methods, not one alone. The argument that both Gadamer and Gilligan are advancing is that we should accept these alternative practices as equally valid.

Weber's analysis of the evolution of legal thought leads to a similar conclusion. The hegemony of the impartial observer and the rule of law is unquestioned; other legal practices are marginalized and devalued. But this is not the whole story. Although devalued in theory, these alternative legal practices are nevertheless utilized; they form the basis of a significant number of decisions in our legal system. In his analysis Weber documents the continued existence of substantive justice in the Western legal tradition. An analysis of contemporary legal practices could add to this list: family courts and adjudication through mediation are examples of legal practices that deviate from the impartiality model. In addition, some Western democracies have adopted a kind of hybrid legal system to deal with the particular situation of native peoples.[7] What these practices reveal is that courts arrive at decisions using methods that include, but are not limited to, the impartiality model. And, most significantly, these decisions have legitimacy in our legal and political system; the existence of multiple paths to legal judgments does not diminish the legitimacy of those judgments.

What I am arguing here is that if we look at what we actually do – in epistemology, morality, and the law – we can learn a valuable lesson. If we look beyond the ideology of impartiality, we see that, in practice, multiple paths to truth exist in each of these areas. We experience truth outside the realm of logic; we act morally on considerations other than abstract justice; and legal decisions are grounded in considerations other than impartial justice. We already engage in these activities; we recognize their legitimacy in practice if not in theory. My argument is that making this recognition explicit and, specifically, granting these practices theoretical as well as practical legitimacy can lead to a new understanding of epistemology, morality, and the law. This is an understanding, furthermore, that will displace the hegemony of the impartiality model. In a Wittgensteinian spirit I am arguing that we should look at what we do rather than what the philosophers say we should do.

A new legal game

In a discussion of the implications of her approach for legal discourse, Gilligan states:

> We are in a new game whose parameters have not been spelled out, whose values are not very well known. We are at the beginning of a process of inquiring, in which the methods themselves will have to be re-examined because the old methods are from the old game. (Gilligan et al. 1985: 45)

To illustrate the parameters of this "new game," Gilligan returns to an example she used in *In a Different Voice*. Studies of the moral development of children frequently measure development by employing a device known as the Heinz dilemma. The dilemma is this: Heinz's wife will die unless she receives an expensive drug that Heinz cannot afford; the druggist who has the drug will not sell it for less than the full price. The child is then asked: should Heinz steal the drug? In her book Gilligan analyses the response of two 11-year-olds to the Heinz dilemma – Jake and Amy. Jake gives the "right" answer to the dilemma – that is, the answer that demonstrates the highest level of moral development on moral psychologist Lawrence Kohlberg's scale. Jake abstracts himself from the particulars of Heinz's case and concludes that there are two moral principles involved: the value of life and the value of property. Since life necessarily takes precedence over property, the "right" answer to the Heinz dilemma is that Heinz should steal the drug. Significantly, Jake arrives at his decision by appealing to the logic of math. Gilligan notes:

> Fascinated by the power of logic, this eleven-year-old boy locates truth in math, which, he says is "the only thing that is totally logical." Considering the moral dilemma to be "sort of like a math problem with humans," he sets it up as an equation and proceeds to work out the solution. (1982: 26)

Amy takes a different tack. Instead of abstracting from the particulars of the case, Amy wants to know more about it. She asks: Does

Heinz love his wife? Has he tried talking to the druggist? Could he borrow the money? She also inquires about the consequences: If Heinz steals the drug and goes to jail, what will happen to his wife? Gilligan comments: "Seeing in the dilemma not a math problem with humans but a narrative of relationships that extends over time," Amy's moral judgment follows a different line (1982: 28). Later, commenting on the legal implications of these responses, Gilligan argues that instead of looking for one "right" solution to legal dilemmas by abstracting from concrete situations (Jake's approach), we should look carefully at the situation to see how we could balance justice and care. Jake's solution exemplifies the law as it is, Gilligan concludes, Amy's the law as it could be (Gilligan et al. 1985: 51–3).

On the basis of the foregoing analysis, I would amend Gilligan's conclusion slightly. Gilligan is correct that Jake's solution exemplifies the law as it is, while Amy's does not. Jake's solution conforms to the dominant legal ideology of the impartial observer, while Amy's violates that ideology. But it does not follow that Amy's position is absent from contemporary legal practice. Attention to particularity and uniqueness, a consideration of consequences, are not infrequently aspects of legal decisions. The relevant point is that they are not accorded the legitimacy of the reigning ideology. According these practices legitimacy as Gilligan advocates, however, can lead to a new understanding of legal practice.[8]

A number of feminist legal theorists have explored the legal implications of Gilligan's work, attempting to define the "new legal game" that she theorizes. In an analysis of the logic of Amy's approach, Carrie Menkel-Meadow comments that Amy "fights the hypo" – that is, that she resists the hypothesizing of the situation that will lead to the "right" answer (1985: 46). This comment has particular significance in legal discourse. Law students are taught to think like Jake, to treat legal / moral dilemmas as "sort of like a math problem with humans." They are also taught that Amy's line of reasoning represents poor legal reasoning. Attention to the concrete and the particular, "fighting the hypo," represents the epitome of sloppy thinking in legal discourse. It is defined, in Weber's terms, as primitive and irrational.

In her discussion of legal discourse, Gilligan offers another example that clarifies the nature of the "new legal game" she is advocating. She describes the conflict between a little girl and a little boy who are playing together. The little girl wants to play the "neighbor game," and the little boy wants to play the "pirate game." The resolution to the conflict suggested by the little boy is to choose one of the two games; the little girl, on the other hand, wants to play a "pirate-next-door game." Gilligan's point is that integrating Amy's voice into legal discourse does not entail choosing one voice over another but, rather, transforming both discourses (Gilligan et al. 1985: 85).

This conclusion is important. Gilligan is very clear in this passage that her goal is integration, not replacement. She wants to integrate elements of the care voice into the justice voice, not obliterate it. Central to this integration is recognizing the legitimacy of the care voice as another, equally legitimate moral voice. What Gilligan is not clear about, however, is the radical character of the change she is advocating. Gilligan's suggestion of a "new legal game" is transformative, in that it suggests that there is no one right answer to any legal / moral problem, but that every situation must be explored in its particularity. Gilligan's example of the two children playing suggests that justice and care can be integrated in legal practice, and that they should be accorded equal legitimacy. Her Jake and Amy example goes even further by suggesting that what hegemonic legal discourse characterizes as "bad" (irrational, primitive) legal reasoning might be precisely the solution to the shortcomings of that discourse. Both these positions constitute heresy for the ideology of the rule of law. They deconstruct its fundamental assumptions and open up an alternative epistemology.

The pressing task for feminist legal theory at this juncture is to formulate strategies to displace the hegemony of the justice voice and to articulate and legitimize an alternative. An analysis of feminist legal theory reveals two strategies that attempt to achieve this goal. The first is an integrative strategy that is employed by most contemporary feminist legal theorists. As Weber pointed out, the impartiality model on which the legal system purportedly rests has never described the totality of legal practice. Our legal system includes elements that are not consistent with the impartiality model. Although these elements are not accorded the legitimacy of the hegemonic model, it is nevertheless the case that we can appeal to these marginalized elements in order to displace the hegemony of the impartiality model and gradually effect change. The strategy of many contemporary feminist legal theorists thus involves pointing to already existing elements in legal practice and arguing that we should legitimize what we already do. Weber pointed out the persistence of "irrational and primitive" elements in the law. Common law and demands for substantive justice violate the impartiality norm, thereby challenging its hegemony; these elements can be employed to destabilize that hegemony. One way of conceptualizing this strategy is to point out that in the law, as in every other field, opposites inhabit each other; what feminists call the care voice has always existed in opposition to the justice voice. Acknowledging this can lead to its displacement.

A second, more radical strategy has also emerged: fashioning arguments that explicitly challenge the epistemological grounding of the discourse of impartiality. The ideology of the rule of law declares that there is one, true morality – the impartial justice voice – and that this morality grounds and legitimizes our legal system. The approach suggested by Gilligan declares, by contrast, that there is more than one path to moral truth, that we choose particular moral arguments because they are appropriate to particular moral situations. I have argued that this approach effectively deconstructs the justice voice, because it challenges the unitary definition of legal truth. But this challenge is rarely made explicit by the feminist legal theorists who follow the first strategy. They claim instead that they are merely attempting to integrate the care voice with the justice voice. The second strategy, however, seeks to displace the justice voice by explicitly formulating an alternative paradigm and rejecting the grounding concepts of the justice paradigm.

Both strategies have their advantages and liabilities. The first strategy has the advantage of appealing to existing legal practices. Advocates of this strategy can thus act as "outsiders within," employing accepted legal arguments and strategies to achieve their goals. They can argue that there are already elements in the law that deviate from the impartiality model, and that we should recognize and legitimize those elements. The liability of this strategy, however, is that it tends to perpetuate the hegemony of the justice voice by casting the care voice as simply "different" rather than as a radical displacement. Like Gilligan, the advocates of this strategy fail to acknowledge that legitimizing multiple paths to legal truth is a radical act that effectively deconstructs the hegemony of the impartiality model. The second strategy, on the other hand, has the advantage of revealing the liabilities of the justice voice by suggesting a radical alternative. Its liability, however, is that it can be, and is, dismissed as incomprehensible and dangerous because it challenges the hegemonic discourse so explicitly. It literally cannot be understood in terms of that discourse and thus is frequently rejected outright.

One of the best examples of the first strategy is Mary Shanley's discussion in "Fathers' rights, mothers' wrongs?" (1995). Examining the argument for unwed father's rights, Shanley asserts that basing these rights on gender neutrality is misleading, because both the biological and the social condition of mothers and fathers is different; gender-neutral rules can thus perpetuate gender inequality. Shanley makes a strong argument for a contextualized approach to the problem, an approach that puts "the lived relationship between parents and between parents and child, not the rights of the individual alone, at the center of the analysis in parental claims" (1995: 96). Several aspects of Shanley's analysis are significant. Her call for attention to the particular and the concrete, the "lived relationship" of the persons involved, can be accommodated within our existing legal system, although it violates the impartiality model. Family law is an arena of law in which particularity is already institutionalized.[9] Although Shanley is arguing for an acknowledgment and extension of this attention to the concrete, it is quite clear from her argument that she is appealing to already existing legal practice. In addition, she points out that the very aims of the impartiality model – gender equality – cannot be achieved by adherence to that model. This is a version of an argument that is becoming increasingly common in the feminist literature: that treating unequals as equals perpetuates inequality. Another way of putting this is that in order to achieve the substantive goal of the impartiality model, we must deviate from the formal criteria of that model. Shanley notes:

> Only by taking account of the interpersonal dependency, reciprocity, and responsibility involved in family relationships will we be able to approach a world dedicated to achieving both lived equality between men and women and committed parents for every child. (1995: 96)

Other feminist theorists have explored similar themes. Carrie Menkel-Meadow (1985) argues that the trend toward mediation as a means of resolving conflict is an "Amy" aspect of our legal system. Eva Kittay (1995), engaging in what she calls a "dependency critique," argues that the Family and Medical Leave Act of 1993 acknowledges a central fact of human life: that all of us, at some point in the life cycle, are dependent on others. This acknowledgment flies in the face of the norm of the autonomous individual on which our legal system rests. But as powerful as these arguments are in certain respects, they also reveal the liability of this strategy. The appeal to the care voice as "different" is, ultimately, unsatisfactory. A common theme of these arguments is that these different voices are exceptions to the rule. None of these theorists claim that particularity and concreteness should constitute an equally valid – much less the dominant – mode of legal discourse. They implicitly acknowledge what Weber's analysis reveals: that references to the particular and the concrete are necessarily devalued in legal discourse. "True" justice is impartial, unbiased, and transcends the particular.

The current debate over affirmative action is perhaps the best illustration of this devaluation of a "different" approach. The premise of affirmative action legislation is that, in order to make up for past inequalities, we must – temporarily and reluctantly – refer to the particulars of persons, specifically gender and race, to distribute rewards in our society. The explicit assumption of these arguments, however, is that we will "return" to the impartiality model once this temporary and unfortunate aberration has been corrected. There are two missing elements in this argument. First, there is no assertion that references to the particular and the concrete that constitute affirmative action legislation are and should be a valid part of legal reasoning; such references are, on the contrary, assumed to be temporary and aberrant. Second, there is no acknowledgment that there is no impartiality norm to return *to*. It was the explicit biases of our society's reward distribution that caused gender and racial hierarchy in the first place; impartiality has never been the norm in reward distribution. Yet the myth persists. The notion that we must "return" to the norm of "the best person for the job" is at the center of the affirmative action debate.

One of the key elements of the integrative approach of the first strategy is the goal of achieving substantive justice for women. Weber claimed that appeals to substantive justice must necessarily deviate from formal, rational legal practices. Feminist legal theory is an excellent example of this thesis. In order to rectify these injustices against women, many feminist legal theorists have turned to the care voice theorized by Gilligan. They argue for a new definition of differences, for attention to particularity and context, and for a relational rather than an autonomous conception of self. But most of these writers are reluctant to completely abandon the hegemonic legal model. Thus they follow Weber in finding other approaches within existing legal practice or, alternatively, find ways to join the two approaches. Few of these theorists acknowledge, however, that integrating different approaches with the hegemonic model radically changes that model. The hegemonic model cannot accommodate other equally valid approaches. Specifically, it cannot accommodate appeals to substantive justice; such appeals are defined as primitive and irrational. Suggesting such an approach without acknowledging this fact thus frequently results in confusion. A good example of this is the work of Ann Scales. Scales rejects the "citadel of objectivity" that informs legal practice. She then argues that "legality should have certain qualities," and that "fairness can exist without objectivity" (1986: 1402). She wants to replace "abstract universality" with "concrete universality" (1986: 1388). She concludes: "The feminist legal standard for equality is altogether principled in requiring commitment to finding the moral crux of matters before the court" (1986: 1403). Exactly how this is to be accomplished, however, remains vague.[10]

Both the advantages and the liabilities of the integrative approach are revealed in the most ambitious attempt to rethink legal discourse along feminist lines: Martha Minow's *Making All the Difference* (1990). The thesis of Minow's book is that we should shift the legal paradigm we use to conceive of difference from a focus on the distinctions between people to a focus on relationships within which we notice and draw distinctions (1990: 15). Minow attacks the central presupposition of our legal system's approach to differ- ence – that there is an objective, neutral standard of normality from which differences can be assessed. Against this, Minow argues, first, that no differences are pre-given, that all are embedded in social relationships, and second, that the allegedly neutral, normal standard of the status quo is biased in favor of white males. She makes it clear that what she calls her "social-relations approach" amounts to a "profound challenge to conventional legal understandings" (1990: 217), that it may "threaten the very idea of law as authoritative and commanding" (1990: 224). In one of the strongest statements of her position she argues:

> Forging ways out of the difference dilemma requires remaking institu- tions so that they do not establish one norm that places the burden of difference on those who diverge from it. It means eliminating the attribution of inferiority to people on the basis of their difference from the norms established within traditional social practices. (1990: 94)

Minow acknowledges that such a radical paradigm shift would not be easy to accomplish. Rights discourse, she concedes, is deeply embedded in our society. Abandoning it raises difficult questions about which claims will be pursued and how (1990: 298); it also involves a profound change in our concept of individualism (1990: 228). As a way of coping with these difficulties, Minow proposes what amounts to a rapprochement between a rights approach and the relational approach she is championing. Early in the book she declares: "I do not reject all that the prior frames of thought have offered; I suggest a dialectical approach connecting a renewed interest in relationships to the prior frameworks that have emphasized right and distinctions between people" (1990: 15). As her argument progresses, she gives examples of how we can embed rights in relationships, thus integrating the two approaches. In conclusion, she claims that her goal has been not to abandon the rhetoric of rights, but to reclaim and reinvent rights (1990: 307). She argues that we must remake rights discourse so that it does not re-create the differences etched by prejudice and misunderstandings into the structure of our institutions (1990: 228).[11]

Minow's argument is compelling. It forces us fundamentally to rethink the concept of difference in legal practices. But it nevertheless stops short of what is required for a new legal epistemology of differences. Minow wants to remake rights discourse by integrating a relational approach. The problem with her strategy is that rights discourse cannot be remade by integrating elements with which it is incompatible. What is required is displacement, not integration. The "alternative" perspective of care cannot be integrated *as* an alternative but, rather, must be incorporated as an equally valid element. This requires completely reconceptualizing the epistemology of rights discourse. Minow's argument must be pushed a step further, so that it explicitly challenges the central element of the epistemology of rights discourse: singularity.

Examples of the second strategy are more difficult to cite. This is not surprising. Given the hegemonic status of the impartiality model, outright challenges to its dominance are problematic. The impartiality model defines what constitutes a proper legal argument; thus radically different arguments will necessarily be labeled incoherent. The hegemonic moral / legal paradigm establishes clear guidelines for right and wrong legal judgments. Deviations from that standard do not make sense, because the paradigm defines what "sense" is in legal discourse. As one theorist puts it, "One cannot at the same moment speak difference and speak coherently" (Haber 1994: 124). Another problematic aspect of an outright challenge to the hegemonic discourse is that this discourse defines alternatives as reactionary, as retreats to a primitive and / or inferior position. Weber labeled appeals to substantive justice "primitive" and "irrational"; Kohlberg defined the "different voice" as a lower level of moral development; the tradition of Western philosophy has labeled the "feminine" approach of connection and relationships as incapable of true moral judgment. Some feminists have even adopted this argument. Feminist critics of the advocacy of the difference voice in moral theory have claimed that emphasizing the traditional moral virtues of women perpetuates, rather than eradicates, women's moral inferiority.

Advocates of the first strategy frequently describe individuals as dependent and needy, embedded in specific relationships and requiring the specific care and attention that the care voice epitomizes. This concept of the individual flies in the face of the autonomous agent that is the basis of the paradigm of impartiality. The contrast between these two conceptions of the individual is muted in the first strategy. In the second strategy, however, it takes center stage. The second strategy's explicit challenge to the hegemony of the impartiality model is rooted in the deconstruction of the autonomous individual that grounds this paradigm. The autonomous individual who forms the basis of social contract theory likewise constitutes the rationalized legal system that Weber has described. Without this individual, the system cannot function.

The paradigm of the autonomous agent of the legal system functions on both sides of that system. First, this paradigm assumes the impartiality of the state's representatives in the legal process, particularly the judge and the jury. The narrative constructed by this paradigm assumes that these actors in the legal drama can remove themselves from the particularity of the situation and apply abstract, universal legal principles to individual cases. Second, the paradigm assumes that individuals charged with crimes are autonomous, in the sense that they are responsible for their actions. The presumption is that it is the individual alone who is responsible for actions committed; the task of the law is only to determine whether these actions are criminal or not. Although the particular situation or socialization of the individual may be cited as an extenuating circumstance, such factors are defined as peripheral rather than constitutive.

Elements of a challenge to the autonomous individual are implicit in the first strategy of feminist legal theorists. The caring self of Gilligan's different voice neither can nor wants to abstract herself from the particulars of her moral situation. Gilligan's discussion of the contrast between the voices of Amy and Jake illustrates this difference. For the Amy voice, the particulars of a moral situation are constitutive, not peripheral. The caring, connected moral self cannot separate who she "really" is from the social and familial forces that constitute her. Furthermore, when Amy places herself in the position of judge, she wants to build on the connectedness that defines her sense of self, not abandon it. The profound lack of fit between the two conceptions of the individual illustrates another respect in which the care voice contains the seeds of the deconstruction of the impartiality paradigm, defeating the project of integration.

The concept of the individual that informs the second strategy is even further removed from the ideal of the autonomous agent. Advocates of this strategy portray individuals in a society, and particularly women, as constituted by the play of social forces. This is a conception of the individual that does not fit into hegemonic legal discourse. Let me give an example. Lisa Parker (1995) analyzes the situation of women who consent to cosmetic surgery. She probes the question of whether the cultural context of female beauty impugns women's ability to give informed consent to cosmetic surgery. What, she asks, does consent mean in this situation? If we argue that women are not *really* consenting, we are treating them as victims, not autonomous agents; if we argue that they do consent, then we ignore the powerful role of social forces in the imposition of a standard of feminine beauty. The whole issue simply does not fit into the model that the law provides. It demands an alternative model of the individual that defines actions contextually and socially.

The clearest example of what I am calling the second strategy is Andrea Dworkin and Catherine MacKinnon's attempt to pass an injunction that defines pornography as a civil crime against women. Dworkin and MacKinnon do not offer arguments that "make sense" in hegemonic legal discourse. Their definition of pornography violates two of the pillars of the concept of the individual that grounds our legal theory and practice: the attribution of individual, linear causality and the right of the autonomous individual to privacy. Although their project has failed in the sense that it has not been enacted as law, this failure is, in another sense, indicative of its success: it confirms the revolutionary challenge that it poses. In one sense, the courts that have ruled their injunction unconstitutional are correct: it *does* threaten the fundamentals of our legal system. But it also highlights the limitations of that system. Women as a group are materially harmed by the existence of pornography in our society. Yet our legal system provides no remedy for this harm, because it cannot be traced in a direct causal line to the specific actions of an individual agent. This alone constitutes a serious indictment of the limitations of our system. But perhaps even more disturbing is the injunction's suggestion that the individual who consumes pornography, the individual whose privacy and rights are at the very center of our legal system, may be causing harm by engaging in this protected activity.

Dworkin and MacKinnon's injunction reveals the limitations of a legal system rooted in the concept of the abstract, autonomous individual and the actions directly caused by that individual. Their work also reveals that, in order to transcend these limitations, we must, in effect, transcend the legal system itself. It is not surprising, then, that their actions have provoked such a violent reaction in the legal community, and that no comparable challenges have been launched. From this perspective, it appears that the first strategy has a better chance of changing legal practice in the United States. Such a conclusion must be qualified. Without radical challenges such as that of Dworkin and MacKinnon, the severe limitations of hegemonic legal discourse would not be evident. From an epistemological perspective it is clear that integrating the care voice with the justice voice necessitates a deconstruction of the hegemonic paradigm. Specifically, it necessitates the rejection of a single path to legal truth and a redefinition of the autonomous individual. But advocates of the integrative approach are not as explicit about these implications as they should be. Radical challenges to the paradigm, even if they fail, are thus crucial, because they highlight its limitations and the necessity of its transformation.

An alternative moral epistemology: multiple voices

In his study of moral development, Lawrence Kohlberg (1984) advanced a model composed of six stages, ranging from the simple moral conceptions characteristic of young children to culmination in the highest level of morality: moral decisions made on the basis of abstract, universal principles (stage 6). Kohlberg's model is decidedly hierarchical and monolithic: on his account, stage 6 is simply what true morality *is*; the other stages are defined as inferior and, in a strict sense, not truly moral. Although not a philosopher, Kohlberg succinctly summarizes the hegemonic moral epistemology of Western thought: true morality is single, abstract, and principled; "different" moral perspectives are ruled out by definition.

Carol Gilligan challenged this tradition with her advocacy of a "different" moral voice. Her stated goal was deceptively simple: to legitimize the moral voice of women and accord it equal validity with the justice voice. Gilligan's argument, however, has implications that far exceed her limited intention. She opened up moral epistemology to an entirely new perspective, a perspective that could incorporate nonhierarchical difference. In an epistemological sense, Gilligan is wrong: the difference voice cannot be integrated into our existing moral epistemology because it violates its premises. It has been my argument that feminists should acknowledge and build on the alternative moral epistemology implicit in the different voice, rather than continue the discussion of the relationship between justice and care.[12]

I indicated at the outset that theorizing an alternative moral epistemology involves two related problems: first, developing strategies for displacing the hegemony of the dominant voice, and second, deciding how to choose among moral voices in a particular moral situation. My answer to the first problem revolved around the argument that we should acknowledge and legitimize what we already do in the moral sphere – that is, adjudicate moral questions using a variety of paths to moral truth. It is my contention that such an acknowledgment would transform moral epistemology by recognizing not one or even two paths to moral truth, but many. I have concentrated here on the first problem because it is a necessary first step. Unless we can alter the moral landscape to include a multiplicity of nonhierarchical moral voices, the second problem cannot even be addressed. It cannot be ignored, however. If there are many paths, rather than one path, to moral truth, then the question of how we choose the appropriate path for a particular moral situation is crucial.

In his epistemological investigations, Gadamer argued that different spheres of understanding have different criteria of truth. Toulmin argued that the "Court of Reason" can be approached by many paths. It is significant, though, that neither theorist addresses what I am here calling the second problem: how to choose the appropriate path to truth.

But although Gadamer does not explicitly discuss the issue of how we decide which path to truth is appropriate in a particular situation, an answer to this question is implicit in his work: we already know which path to choose. In his discussion of different experiences of truth, Gadamer employs the example of art. He argues that our experience of truth when we encounter a great work of art is very different from that which we experience upon completion of a mathematical calculation. How do we know this? How do we know when we stand in front of the Mona Lisa that we should not take out our calculators? Or when we are solving a mathematical equation that we should? We know because we live in a society that makes these choices for us. Embedded in what Gadamer calls our prejudices and Wittgenstein calls our language games is the knowledge that mathematical calculations will not reveal the beauty of the Mona Lisa, nor will aesthetic considerations allow us to solve a mathematical problem. Only rarely does the choice of the appropriate path to truth even enter our consciousness. Once more, it is simply what we do.

These insights are applicable to the moral sphere as well. We know that certain moral / legal situations require careful attention to context and particular circumstances, while others require considerations of abstract justice. We know, for example, that in a child custody case in family court the particulars of all the participants' situations must be carefully attended to. We also know that exclusive appeals to abstract principles of justice will not be appropriate; Jake's approach will not work, but Amy's will. It does not follow, however, that abstract principles of justice have no place in the moral/legal landscape. It is appropriate to ask prospective jurors whether they have a connection to the case at hand, to recuse judges whose bias in a particular situation will be detrimental. Abstract principles of justice played a different role in the O. J. Simpson trial than they did in the Timothy McVeigh trial; there was much discussion about these differences. The point is that although there is difference and disagreement about these issues, we are nevertheless capable of negotiating these moral questions by appealing to our common moral understandings. We know that different moral considerations are appropriate in different situations. Sometimes these choices are made with little reflection; sometimes serious deliberation is needed; and gray areas abound. But it is nevertheless the case that our moral education provides us with the tools by which we navigate these moral waters.

What I am arguing is, again, that we should look at what we do for an answer to this question. Which path to moral truth is appropriate in a particular situation is something that the members of a particular society already know. When I was a child, my father used to make jokes about our family being governed as a democracy. Even as an eight-year-old, I knew this was a joke and why. I also knew that there were certain circumstances under which appeals to equality within the family were appropriate. We recognize spheres of morality just as we recognize experiences of truth: by appeal to our common knowledge.

It should be obvious from the foregoing, however, that any appeal to the moral practices of our society must be significantly qualified in a feminist context. The prejudices of our society have defined the moral considerations of women as inferior to those of men. They have dictated that even by the standards of the alleged neutrality of the justice voice, it is "just" to treat women as second-class citizens, excluding them from equal participation in the economic and political spheres. The contemporary feminist movement is a protest against these prejudices, a refusal to accept the inferior status conferred on women. In the moral sphere, Gilligan's argument protests the prejudice against women's style of moral reasoning. Her approach illustrates that for feminism to succeed, it must alter the boundaries of language games, protest the prejudices that define the inferior status of women.

What Gilligan and other feminist moral theorists have argued is that the moral spheres that already exist should be acknowledged as legitimate and accorded equality with the hegemonic discourse of the justice voice. Like the methodological arguments I cited in the last chapter, I think this argument can be characterized as a kind of "outsider within" approach. It is an argument that pushes the boundaries of existing language games, but it does not abandon them altogether. Discussions of the care voice are appeals to regard this existing moral practice in a different light. Feminists are questioning the prejudices that devalue this voice while at the same time appealing to our common understandings of the moral voices that constitute our moral practices. Thus the feminist argument takes place both inside and outside those practices: it appeals to our common understandings of moral language games while at the same time changing the boundaries of those language games; it both intersects with and transforms the moral language game.

Examining moral practices in terms of the operation of moral language games can also throw light on another obstacle to the advocacy of multiple moral voices: the specter of moral anarchy. It is often argued that acknowledging multiple moral truths will result in moral chaos, a world in which any individual can claim that his or her moral voice is as legitimate and as valid as that of anyone else. I think it is possible to dismiss this fear on the grounds that it is based on a misunderstanding of the operation of moral language games. Acquiring a moral voice is a social and interactive process. Moral voices develop in tandem with selfhood itself; both are social processes that are constituted by participation in a community of values.[13] On this understanding of moral voice, the proverbial axe murderer who claims legitimacy for his or her moral voice can be quite easily dismissed. This claim is not the product of the community of values that constitutes and legitimizes moral voices; it is ungrounded and hence illegitimate. On the other hand, the mother who stands up in a court of law and claims that the well-being of her child demands an exception to the applicable legal statute most likely will be heard. Her voice, the moral voice of maternal care, comes out of a community of value both recognized and legitimate.

Modernist moral theory offers a reassuring bulwark against moral anarchy: there is one right path to moral truth constituted by adherence to abstract universal moral principles. Once we abandon this conception, reassurances are hard to come by. We live in a world of multiple moral paths and truths. We negotiate this world by relying on our established moral language games and the moral habits we have acquired. Some of those moral habits – specifically, the hegemony of the justice voice – devalue women's moral practices. As feminists, thus, we will resist some of those moral habits, contesting the hegemony of the justice voice and arguing for the legitimacy of other voices. The form of our resistance, however, is circumscribed by those language games and the permeability of their boundaries. It is a delicate process; it involves the simultaneous employment of apparent opposites: connection and transformation. But in a world devoid of moral and epistemological absolutes, it is the most effective strategy we have.

5

Backgrounds and Riverbeds:
Feminist Reflections

The task of displacing the hegemony of the justice voice in Western moral theory is closely linked to another, even more difficult task: displacing the hegemony of the dominant tradition of Western epistemology. This task is fundamental to completing the arguments of the last two chapters: developing a new methodology to accommodate differences and legitimizing more than one path to moral truth. Unless feminists can alter the definition of "Truth" itself, what I am calling the third strategy cannot succeed.

I have argued that the first and second strategies of contemporary feminism in their attempts to either erase or emphasize difference have failed to displace the unitary epistemology of Western thought but, rather, have conformed to it. The third strategy, by contrast, demands a new conception of truth, an explicitly anti-foundational epistemology. It is a conception that must challenge every element of hegemonic Western epistemology. It is significant that challenges to this epistemology began to emerge in the second strategy. Descartes' disembodied knower is challenged by the concept of the relational self. The claim that truth can be achieved only through adherence to one rational, universal method is challenged by the care voice, the feminist standpoint, and women's ways of knowing. Other aspects of an alternative epistemology, furthermore, are emerging in many areas of twentieth-century thought, both feminist and nonfeminist. Discussions of the parameters of an anti-foundational epistemology appear in the work of such disparate thinkers as Rorty, Gadamer, Foucault,

Wittgenstein, Butler, Code, and Haraway. These discussions have begun to have a significant impact on epistemology. But they have also generated charges of "unbridled relativism," chaos, and epistemological anarchy.

In the following I focus on one aspect of the problem of defining an anti-foundational epistemology that is crucial for the feminist project. My argument is rooted in three premises that are shared by most of the theorists cited above: that every society requires a ground for meaning that makes language intelligible, that this ground is ungrounded in the sense that it lacks universal validity, and that this ground provides a stable foundation for meaning that extends over time. It is my contention that these premises give rise to a set of unique problems for feminist theory. If feminists assume with the anti-foundationalists that truth statements are grounded in social meanings (or language games, or prejudices, or discourses), then their theories, unlike those of nonfeminists, must confront the inferiority of women that those social meanings dictate. The ungrounded ground of anti-foundational thought is synonymous with hegemonic masculinist discourse. It is, from a feminist perspective, both the ground of all possible meaning in that society and at the same time precisely the set of understandings that must be altered if feminism is to succeed. Nonfeminist anti-foundational epistemologists, furthermore, do not offer much guidance when it comes to how those social meanings change or might be changed. They do, however, tell us how change cannot occur. The anti-foundationalist cannot advocate changing social meanings by claiming that they are in some absolute sense "wrong" and replacing them with understandings that are "true" and "right." If social meanings define what is "true," it follows that only other social meanings can define another truth that would, in turn, define another social structure. But this is not very helpful for the feminist, because it is exceedingly vague and, further, because other social meanings will tend to reinforce rather than redress the inferior status of women. In the absence of an independent truth or reality to which we can appeal, this would seem to leave feminism in a vicious circle from which there is no escape.

Attempting to articulate an escape from this circle is the subject of this chapter.[1] My vehicle is a concept that, in different forms, has been prominent in twentieth-century thought: what John Searle has most recently called the "Background." Although Searle's definition is not the only or even the best definition of this concept, it is a useful place to start in describing it. Searle defines the Background as that which enables linguistic interpretation to take place; it is the recognition and acceptance of a body of facts by the members of a society in which they are operative. This acceptance constitutes these facts; if it ceases, the facts themselves cease to exist (1995: 117, 132). Searle freely admits that his concept of the Background is not original. He notes discussions of the Background by the later Wittgenstein, Bourdieu, Hume, and Nietzsche. I would go further and claim that discussions of what Searle calls the Background pervade late twentieth-century thought. Gadamer's discussion of prejudice, Oakeshott's analysis of habit, Wittgenstein's language games, and, in a different vein, Foucault's concept of *episteme*, are all versions of the Background. The effort to define the status of the agreements that both allow and constitute social life has become a major preoccupation of contemporary philosophy.

Discussions of the Background by this disparate array of thinkers is a profoundly important development in epistemology. The theorists of the Background argue that without a core of agreed-upon assumptions about both the social and the natural worlds (or, for that matter, even a distinction between them), human social life would be impossible; human intelligibility requires common understandings. Furthermore, theories of the Background offer a viable epistemological alternative to two equally unacceptable positions: absolutism and nihilism. The dichotomy between these two positions has plagued contemporary philosophical discussions and has been especially problematic in feminism. Theorists of the Background effectively displace this binary by asserting a nonfoundational foundation. They define a set of fundamental beliefs that are not absolute; these beliefs vary among societies and change over time within societies. Yet these beliefs provide a secure foundation for meaning and understanding: they produce not nihilism, but the very possibility of intelligibility.

My most significant reason for focusing on the Background, however, is that the Background determines not only the possibility of intelligibility, but also the possibility of changing the ground of that intelligibility. If the Background defines the grounds for the constitution of meaning within a society, then feminists who want to change these grounds must begin with an analysis of the Background. We must thoroughly understand the nature and operation of those grounds if we are to formulate strategies for displacing the hegemony they define. Furthermore, focusing on the Background reveals that two strategies frequently employed by feminist epistemologists will be ineffective: attempting to define the final "truth" of social reality and attempting to demolish the Background outright. Attention to the Background reveals, rather, that feminist strategies must be simultaneously incremental, connective, and transformative. Our goal must be to shift the grounds of the Background, to redefine truth in terms that both connect to Background assumptions and at the same time begin the process of displacing those assumptions.[2]

A feminist analysis of theories of the Background, however, must begin with significant qualifications. From a feminist perspective the twentieth-century discussion of the Background is disturbing on a number of levels. First, it is a discussion that occurs in an orbit untouched by feminist analysis. I have argued that discussions of the Background are a central aspect of contemporary philosophical thought. But feminists have not been a part of these discussions. Analyses of the Background are gender-blind: feminist issues are not just marginalized, they are invisible. While philosophers may pay lip service to feminist approaches in many instances, when it comes to "serious" philosophical issues like epistemology, feminist concepts quickly disappear.[3] Second, most, if not all, the philosophers of the Background ignore two issues central to feminist concerns: power and social change. With the notable exception of Foucault, questions of how social facts come to be accepted and the mechanisms by which they are maintained are not even raised. Further, these discussions are by their very nature profoundly conservative. There is almost no discussion of how Background assumptions change, or might be changed, with the aim of constituting a better social world. Finally, and most importantly for feminism, there is no discussion of the Background from an epistemological perspective as a masculinist construction of reality, a social construct that defines and reinforces the hegemony of men.

Despite these significant drawbacks, I think that a feminist reading of the Background provides an opportunity to begin the task of formulating the new epistemology that the third strategy demands. Most Background theorists, especially those with a conservative orientation, ignore issues of gender and power; but this is not a limitation inherent in the concept. Indeed, one could argue that gender and power are necessarily crucial aspects of the Background. One could further argue that exploring society's Background assumptions about gender and power has always been the task of feminist analysis. It is my claim that if we incorporate feminism's insights into the workings of gender and power with the Background theorists' insights into the constitution of meaning, we have the potential to provide a new epistemology for differences.[4]

Theories of the Background

In 1995 one of the pillars of the American philosophical establishment, John Searle, published a book with the ambitious title *The Construction of Social Reality*. His title has an obvious subtext: it is a challenge to the popular late twentieth-century conception that reality is socially constructed. The strongly argued thesis of Searle's book is that there is a reality "out there" that does not require human institutions for its existence, and that this reality – what Searle calls "non-institutional" or "brute facts" – grounds the institutional facts that societies construct. The object of his book is to explain, given the existence of these noninstitutional facts, how institutional facts, facts that exist only because of human agreement, come into being.

I begin my discussion of the Background by focusing on Searle's theory, not because it is the most useful for feminist purposes (Wittgenstein's theory deserves this designation), but, rather, because Searle provides a good illustration of what, in a sense, feminists are up against. Searle embodies the philosophical establishment in Anglo-American philosophy. Although the work of Continental philosophers has proved to be more compatible with feminist concerns, this compatibility has not brought feminism into the mainstream of philosophy, because in most American philosophy departments Anglo-American philosophy is still predominant. Thus Searle's blindness to feminist issues is particularly egregious. In his book Searle analyzes a question that is central to feminist concerns – the distinction between institutional and noninstitutional facts – without once mentioning a feminist issue or perspective. This in itself is a significant statement about the role of feminism in contemporary philosophy and the nature of the problem that feminists must confront.

Searle's basic thesis with regard to institutional facts is that language is constitutive of institutional reality. In his vocabulary, what this means is that institutional facts are ontologically subjective – their existence depends on people's beliefs – but epistemologically objective – they *do* exist. Institutional facts – marriage, war, private property, etc. – must be accepted by a majority if they are to continue in effect; once this acceptance ceases, they are no longer effective (1995: 59ff). It is these institutional facts that form what Searle calls the "Background." The Background performs a number of necessary and vital functions in society: it enables linguistic and perceptual interpretation to take place; it structures consciousness; it temporally extends sequences of experience that come to us with a narrative or dramatic shape; it facilitates expectations and disposes people to certain kinds of behavior (1995: 132–6).

In his discussion of the Background, Searle spends a lot of time grappling with the question of causality. In what sense, he asks, does the Background act as a cause of our behavior? Neither of the established conceptions of causality – rational decision according to rules or brute physical causation – explain the causal mechanisms of the Background. Searle concludes from this that the kind of causality that the Background exerts is unique. It involves developing a set of abilities that are sensitive to specific structures without being constituted by that intentionality. The "rules" that constitute the Background are never self-interpreting or exhaustive; they do not enter consciously or unconsciously into our decision-making process – we just *know* what to do. Searle concludes:

> [I]n learning to cope with social reality, we acquire a set of cognitive abilities that are everywhere sensitive to an intentional structure, and in particular to the rule structures of complex institutions, without necessarily containing representations of the rules of those institutions. (1995: 145)

Thus, it is not the case that individuals master the rules of society, but, rather, that they develop a set of capacities and abilities that render them at home in that society (1995: 147).

One of the conclusions Searle hopes to derive from his analysis is a defense of realism. External realism, he argues, functions as a taken-for-granted part of the Background. Unless we assume external realism, he argues, we cannot understand relevances in the way that we normally do (1995: 182). The effort to communicate in a public language necessarily presupposes a public world in the sense that the "public" exists independent of our representations of it. The price of abandoning this conception of external realism, thus, is the abandonment of normal understanding (1995: 187–9). But, unlike most defenders of realism, Searle does not argue for a "natural" ground for culture. Instead, he asserts that the traditional opposition between biology and culture is suspect. He argues that culture is the form that biology takes; the connection between biology and culture is consciousness and intentionality; the uniqueness of culture is the existence of collective intentionality (1995: 227–8).

Despite Searle's failure to connect any of these issues to gender, his account resonates on several levels from a feminist perspective. An analysis of his approach illustrates how a feminist reading of the Background can supply missing elements as well as turn other elements in a feminist direction. His statement that institutional facts are epistemologically objective and ontologically subjective is difficult to challenge. Pivotal to his argument is the claim that institutional facts do indeed exist, and that the basis for their existence is the social acceptance that constitutes them; looking for any other foundation would misunderstand the nature of those facts. What Searle does not pursue, however, are two important aspects of the ontological subjectivity of institutional facts that would necessarily be central to a feminist analysis: power and change. Searle studiously avoids the issue of how power maintains the status quo and how countervailing power might facilitate change. He does not explore how the "social acceptance" that constitutes institutional facts is established, or how forces that might alter those facts arise. His vision is both monolithic and static. He asserts that "we" agree on these facts without examining who this "we" is, or how this agreement is imposed. The question of how this "we" might change its collective mind is not even raised.

Searle's discussion of causality, although devoid of gender issues, offers interesting possibilities when turned in a feminist direction. A key component of contemporary feminism and an important element in my description of the emergence of the third strategy is the position usually labeled "social constructionism." Feminist social constructionists assert that women are made, not born, and thus that gender and even sex are social, not natural, constructions. I have argued that social constructionism has immensely enriched feminist critiques in the past decades; it has allowed feminists to challenge what have appeared to be biological givens about women's role in society. But it has also raised a serious theoretical problem. If, as the social constructionists argue, we are constituted by social forces, then it would seem to follow that the members of a society would emerge with cookie-cutter sameness. Taken to its logical extreme, social constructionism leads to what some critics have called the problem of the "social dupe." Total determination by cultural forces would obviate the emergence of individual differences; more troublingly, it would even make it impossible to account for social rebels such as feminists.

The title of Searle's book, *The Construction of Social Reality*, is a none-too-subtle attack on social constructionism. It is therefore ironic that Searle's work offers a way around the problem of the social dupe. Searle argues for a unique understanding of the causal mechanism of the Background. Following the "rules" of the Background is not like following the rules of a game; the Background's rules are never self-interpreting or exhaustive. The set of capacities and abilities we develop allow us to feel at home in our society. Our actions in a social setting, thus, do not constitute rote obedience to hard and fast rules but, rather, loosely circumscribed actions that allow for a good deal of latitude and slippage. This conception offers a way of explaining individual differences within a culture without abandoning an understanding of the determining role of cultural forces. Given the importance of this problem for feminist theory, this aspect of Searle's theory of the Background is significant. It illustrates the utility of employing the concept of the Background to address problems that, in other contexts, seem intractable.

Finally, Searle's discussion of the relationship between biology and culture can also be turned to feminist purposes. The point of his discussion is to establish the validity of "external realism" and the priority of brute facts over institutional facts. But his argument can be put to more radical uses. His contention is that the traditional opposition between biology and culture is suspect; he asserts instead that culture is the form that biology takes (1995: 227). What this amounts to is the deconstruction of a central, and deeply gendered, dualism. The biology (nature)/culture dualism has been central to Western thought, coding nature as female and culture as male, defining women as not truly human. It has also been used to define a "natural" role for women based on women's (sexed) biology. Displacing this binarism is very useful in displacing the sex/gender binarism that has caused so much trouble in feminist theory. We might say, paraphrasing Searle, that gender is the form that sex takes; there is no neat division between them.[5]

In the course of elaborating his theory, Searle dismisses Wittgenstein's approach to the Background as inadequate, on the grounds that Wittgenstein does not explore in detail the constitution of institutional facts. But, from a feminist perspective, Wittgenstein's position is more useful than Searle's. Wittgenstein reveals more clearly than Searle the deep-rootedness of the Background. For Wittgenstein, the Background is embedded in the grammar of our language and, ultimately, in what he calls our form of life. Further, and most importantly, Wittgenstein's discussion of justification offers insight into how the Background changes.

At the center of Wittgenstein's discussion of the Background is his claim that our language is grounded not in the universal metanarrative of logic but, rather, in our activity.[6] In *Philosophical Investigations* (1958) Wittgenstein argues that the ultimate justification for our claims to knowledge is not logic, but simply "what we do." "It is what human beings *say* that is true and false; and they agree in the *language* they use. That is not agreement in opinions but in form of life" (1958: §241). And elsewhere, Our concepts rest not on "a seeing on our part; it is our *acting* which lies at the bottom of the language game" (Wittgenstein 1969: §204). Philosophers since Plato have looked for ultimate justifications, complete explanations. What Wittgenstein is advocating, by contrast, is an end to justifications, not in logic but in human activity itself: "What people accept as a justification – is shewn by how they think and live" (1958: §325); "the chain of reasons has an end" (1958: §326). "Our mistake is to look for an explanation where we ought to look at what happens as a 'proto-phenomenon'. That is, where we ought to have said: *this language-game is played*" (1958: §654).

At a crucial point in his argument, Wittgenstein appears to go beyond a description of human activity as the justification for our knowledge and to appeal to a universalistic grounding. His discussion of "general facts of nature" and "natural history" seems to imply that he is not content with the contextual account he has given and is looking for more reliable, universal criteria. But Wittgenstein's definition of these terms does not entail this conclusion. For Wittgenstein, our "natural history" includes not just our biological or "natural" activities, but our linguistic activities as well: "Commanding, questioning, recounting, chatting, are as much a part of our natural history as walking, eating, drinking, playing" (1958: §25). Our language games are as natural to human life as our biological life. Most important, language games literally *give* us a world in which to live; our concepts are part of the fabric of our form of life. Wittgenstein's point in his famous statement "If a lion could talk, we could not understand him" (1958: §223) is not that our biology differs from that of lions but, rather, that a lion's concepts would create a world that we could not comprehend. Wittgenstein summarizes thus:

> I am not saying: if such-and-such facts of nature were different, people would have different concepts (in the sense of a hypothesis). But: if anyone believes that certain concepts are absolutely the correct ones, and that having different ones would mean not realizing something that we realize – then let him imagine certain very general facts of nature to be different from what we are used to, and the formation of

concepts different from the usual ones will become intelligible to him. (1958: §230)

If anything, Wittgenstein's approach here sounds more conservative than Searle's: human activity and human language are inextricably linked in our natural history. But another aspect of the Background emerges in Wittgenstein's discussion of justification in *On Certainty* (1969). The metaphor that Wittgenstein uses to make his argument here is that of the riverbed. It is a complicated metaphor involving shifts and alterations:

> It might be imagined that some propositions, of the form of empirical propositions, were hardened and functioned as channels for such empirical propositions as were not hardened but fluid; and that this relation altered with time, in that fluid propositions hardened, and hard ones became fluid. The mythology may change back into a state of flux, the riverbed of thoughts may shift. (1969: §96–7)

Wittgenstein's description of how this shifting occurs, however, is very ambiguous:

> But I distinguish between the movement of the waters on the river-bed and the shift of the bed itself; though there is not a sharp division of the one from the other. And the bank of the river consists partly of hard rock, subject to no alteration or only to an imperceptible one, partly of sand, which now in one place and now in another gets washed away or deposited. (1969: §98–9)

And, finally,

> All testing, all confirmation and disconfirmation of a hypothesis takes place already within a system. And this system is not a more or less arbitrary and doubtful point of departure for all our arguments: no, it belongs to the essence of what we call an argument. The system is not so much the point of departure as the element in which arguments have their life. (1969: §105)

Wittgenstein's reference to a "mythology," a "world picture" (1969: §162) paints a much more complex picture of the Background than that of Searle. In *Philosophical Investigations* he asserts: "A *picture* held us captive. And we could not get outside it, for it lay in our language and language seemed to repeat it to us inexorably" (1958: §115). Asking whether this mythology, this picture, is true or false is asking the wrong question, because "Above all, it is the substratum of all my inquiry and asserting" (1969: §162). Another way of putting this is that the question of reasons does not have a place in this language game.[7] The picture that structures our thought is not arbitrary, but grounded. The ground, however, is not nature but interconnectedness: "What I hold fast is not *one* proposition but a nest of propositions" (1969: §225). And, finally, "At the foundation of well-founded belief lies belief that is not founded" (1969: §252). Thus

> Giving grounds, however, justifying the evidence, comes to an end; – but the end is not certain propositions striking us immediately as true, i.e., it is not a kind of *seeing* on our part; it is our *acting* which lies at the bottom of the language. (1969: §204)

"At the end of reasons comes *persuasion*" (1969: §612).[8]

Wittgenstein's account of the Background, much more than Searle's, reveals what I see to be the feminist implications of the concept. Both Wittgenstein and Searle emphasize that the Background provides the possibility of meaning in social life, that it is the necessary medium in which understanding takes place. Both emphasize that it is an ungrounded ground, and that it is social agreement that, as Wittgenstein puts it, holds it fast. But Searle, most likely because he fears the encroachment of postmodern nihilism, avoids the question of how the Background changes; his Background does not shift. Wittgenstein is bolder. His riverbed metaphor in *On Certainty* encompasses change, flux, even "mythology." Wittgenstein's position makes clear, however, that accounting for change entails neither arbitrariness nor nihilism. Riverbeds shift slowly, incrementally; the slowness of the change and the complexity of the elements that constitute meaning entail that the process of change does not threaten meaning itself.

I want to draw a number of guidelines for a feminist theory of change from Wittgenstein's theory. The first is an emphasis on connection. The riverbed of meaning in his metaphor shifts not overnight but over time. It changes course eventually because the water flows through an adjacent section of the riverbed, a section connected by rock and sand to the main riverbed. Change is thus effected by connection, not radical relocation. I interpret this to mean that social and linguistic change is a function of the redeployment and redefinition of words and practices that already exist in social life. Social reformers take linguistic tools that are already at their disposal and reemploy them in new areas; they take the familiar and turn it to unfamiliar purposes. The result is new social/linguistic practices.

The second guideline I want to draw belies the seemingly conservative implications of the first. Wittgenstein claims that our concepts give us a world, and that we can apprehend the world only through these concepts. This does not mean that the world and those concepts cannot change. What it means is that changing our concepts means changing our world. Peter Winch puts this point nicely:

> [T]here is no way of getting outside the concepts in terms of which we think of the world. The world *is* for us what is presented through those concepts. That is not to say that our concepts may not change, but when they do, that means that our concept of the world has changed, too. (1958: 15)

The only world we can make any sense of is the world given to us in our concepts. But those concepts are fluid and malleable. We can take concepts from one language game and deploy them in another. We can work at the borders of language games where meaning is less distinct. (Foucault talks about the interstices between discourses.) The point is that changing these concepts on the margins can and does profoundly change our world; it shifts the riverbed onto new rock and sand. But, far from inviting nihilism and chaos, this understanding of social/linguistic change builds the possibility of change into the bedrock of social intelligibility.

Subverting the Background

It should come as no surprise that twentieth-century theorists who have sought to change the social and political order have not been enamored of theories of the Background. On the face of it, the Background is a conservative concept. It assumes that meaning rests on something like tradition – the set of meanings handed down to us from our forefathers (not, significantly, our foremothers). Speaking of language, J. L. Austin once said: "Our common stock of words embodies all the distinctions men have found worth drawing, and the connections they have found worth marking, in the lifetimes of many generations" (1961: 182). This is a good description of the Background. It is not insignificant that one of the most famous theorists of the Background, Edmund Burke, used it to argue against the viability of radical social or political revolution.

Despite its conservative heritage, however, aspects of a theory of the Background appear in oppositional theories, beginning with Marx. One way of interpreting Marx's thought is that he is presenting a detailed description of the Background in capitalist society and the situation it defined for the proletariat. Marx was quite clear that capitalism defined reality for all classes within the social structure. Indeed, he had a lot to say about the constitution of that social reality: the role of ideology, the operation of the superstructure, the role of history in the construction of social consciousness. But his point in doing so, obviously, was quite different from that of a Burke. He wanted to emphasize that the reality created and maintained by capitalism was false, an ideological distortion of true reality. Marx's approach is grounded in the conviction that there is a true social reality that can and must be distinguished from false conceptions.

Marx's theories of the social construction of reality, furthermore, have had far-reaching effects in twentieth-century social and political theory. Social phenomenology, the sociology of knowledge, theories of the relational self, to name a few, all owe a debt to Marx. Many of these theories, however, adopt Marx's concept of the social construction of reality without at the same time accepting his theory of a true, material reality to which it is opposed. In chapter 2 I theorized that there is a reason for this: once one begins to speculate on the social construction of reality, it is only a matter of time until any absolute grounding for that reality will be challenged.[9] Marx's understanding of the social construction of reality was a fertile concept; it bore fruit across a range of disciplines in the twentieth century. But its success also led to the deconstruction of one of its central tenets: the existence of a true, material reality.

Some of the twentieth-century thinkers who have utilized a quasi-Marxist concept of the construction of social reality have done so with the goal of simply describing that reality. Thus, for example, social phenomenologists have offered elaborate descriptions of how reality is constructed, divided, and subdivided into various spheres. These descriptions have been criticized by those who want to carry on the Marxist oppositional tradition as inadequate, because they deny what they define as the purpose of social theory: instituting social change. These critics argue that unless we retain some notion of a "true reality" that opposes social constructions, we cannot formulate oppositional theories. I want to challenge this critique, to argue that theories of the Background can be oppositional without being foundational. Even more, I want to argue that it is only by understanding the Background as an ungrounded ground that we can begin to formulate strategies for social change.

The best place to begin this argument is with the twentieth-century thinker who most clearly illustrates both the oppositional impulse of Marx and the rejection of "true reality": Michel Foucault. Foucault continues the oppositional tradition of Marxism, elaborating and deepening many of Marx's explorations of the construction of social reality, while at the same time abandoning Marx's theoretical grounding in material reality. The results have important implications for formulating an oppositional theory of the Background.[10]

One of the most insightful statements about the Background in the work of Foucault is the passage at the beginning of *The Order of Things* that he quotes from Borges. "A certain Chinese encyclopedia," Borges claims, divides animals into:

(a) belonging to the Emperor, (b) embalmed, (c) tame, (d) sucking pigs, (e) sirens, (f) fabulous, (g) stray dogs, (h) included in the present classification, (i) frenzied, (j) innumerable, (k) drawn with a very fine camelhair brush, (l) *et cetera*, (m) having just broken the water pitcher, (n) that from a long way off look like flies. (1971: xv)

Although Borges's list is not, I think, meant to be taken seriously, Foucault's use of it is very serious. His book is an attempt to provide a classification of the underlying assumptions of Western thought. He defines the elements of the Background in Western thought and, specifically, how significant aspects of the Background have shifted from classical to modern thought. Foucault calls this Background the "*a priori* of thought":

This *a priori* is what, in a given period, delimits in the totality of experience a field of knowledge, defines the mode of being of the objects that appear in that field, provides man's everyday perception with theoretical powers, and defines the conditions in which he can sustain a discourse about things that is recognized to be true. (1971: 158)

Foucault's discussion of the Background, particularly in *The Order of Things*, extends the theory in important respects. First, although elements of his argument are present in other Background theorists, Foucault's interest in the history of the human sciences opens up a new understanding of the Background. He traces how the a priori of thought creates a world for the scientist that excludes other conceptions. His discussion of the discursive constitution of the human sciences, furthermore, fills in the gaps left in Weber's approach. Foucault is more explicit than Weber in defining the human sciences as creating the world that they study through the deployment of the specific discursive matrix that constitutes each science. He thus explains more clearly than Weber how a scientific discourse allows certain kinds of investigations and precludes others.

The second respect in which Foucault's theory of the Background breaks new ground is his discussion of subjectivity. Unlike other theorists of the Background, Foucault locates subjectivity itself in the Background. His argument that discourses create subjects as well as objects moves his theory onto a new epistemological plane. Marx was ambiguous on this point. Although Marx argued that consciousness is historically and materially constituted, he also assumed that this determination could be transcended by rational, scientific thought. Foucault rejects the characterization of the transcendent subject in all its guises. He argues that subjects are discursive products, that we learn how to be a subject by participating in a discourse. But this theory does not entail that we all become social dupes. Resistance, on Foucault's account, is also an element of the constitution of subjectivity. What his theory precludes is an Archimedean point of pure subjectivity that provides a space for critique (Foucault 1982).

Foucault's third innovation is that, despite his oppositional stance, he refuses to privilege any discourse as "true," as the final grounding of social reality. Operating on the assumption that all knowledge is discursively constructed, he defines his task as the explication of the mechanism by which discursive formations are constituted. One aspect of this argument is especially relevant here. In a manner reminiscent of Gadamer and Toulmin, Foucault argues that the Enlightenment is a historically determined discourse, a unique discursive construction, not the one path to truth. Furthermore, Foucault's deconstruction of the key concept of Enlightenment thought, the transcendent subject, gives his critique added force. Although both Gadamer and, to a lesser extent, Gilligan, also reject the Enlightenment's transcendental subject, Foucault's explicit deconstruction of the concept of "man" in *The Order of Things* moves this critique to a new level.

Foucault's theory provides an illustration of the possibilities of an oppositional theory of the Background. If we are looking for a specifically feminist oppositional theory, however, his approach has serious limitations. Foucault's task is to probe the discursive construction of knowledge within the disciplines we call the human sciences and, later, the constitution of the self in the West. Although these probings yield interesting, even startling results, his analysis does not go as deep as those of Searle and Wittgenstein. He explores what it means to make sense in certain areas of social life and in particular disciplines, not what it means to make sense at all. This limitation informs one of the most serious drawbacks of his approach: his blindness to gender. Gendered binaries profoundly structure the elements of sense in Western thought; they span historical periods, informing disparate discourses. They are particularly influential in the human sciences that occupy so much of Foucault's attention. And, most significantly, they quite literally constitute our understanding of the self in the West. Foucault's failure to probe more deeply into the constitution of meaning causes him to "miss" gender almost entirely. This creates a strange lacuna in his analysis, limiting the depth of his perspective.

Finally, Foucault is at best vague on an issue that must be at the forefront of the feminist critique: change. In *The Order of Things* the mechanism by which discourses change what it makes sense to say and, consequently, how reality is constructed is mysterious: discourses change because "counter-sciences" on the margins somehow come to the forefront. How these counter sciences emerge and the mechanism by which they replace the hegemonic science remain unclear. In the essays and interviews collected in *Power/Knowledge* (1980) Foucault discusses the issue of change more directly. He introduces the concept of the "insurrection of subjugated knowledges" (1980: 81) and argues that this is the principal instrument of change. This is a useful concept, and one that is relevant to the formation of a feminist critique of the Background. The experiences of women are, in Foucault's sense, subjugated knowledges; bringing them to the foreground can and does alter what counts as knowledge. But, again, Foucault remains vague on the mechanisms by which these subjugated knowledges alter discursive formations.

This vagueness is also related to Foucault's failure to probe the underlying mechanisms of the Background. Wittgenstein explains how what he calls the riverbed of thought structures what it makes sense to say. He also explains how the underlying assumptions about meaning in a society can gradually change, how, in his metaphor, the riverbed of thought can shift. Foucault does neither. The discourses he describes are hermetically sealed entities. Like Kuhn, he argues that discourses/paradigms are incommensurable. Wittgenstein, by contrast, portrays a world in which basic underlying assumptions constitute meaning itself and undergird particular discourses. Thus, using a Wittgensteinian perspective, we can explain how the existence of basic understandings about, for example, what constitutes a good argument are common to an array of discourses within a particular society.

This is an important insight. Because he does not probe the question of meaning constitution deeply enough, Foucault can only describe change in terms of waiting for the next discourse, whatever it might be, to overthrow the established hegemony of the now-dominant discourse. It is an oddly passive theory of change. Foucault gives us no indication of how we might effect change or, most importantly, steer it in a particular direction. Wittgenstein, by contrast, by providing an understanding of the common grounding for all discourses, gives us a deeper understanding of meaning constitution, one that allows us to understand the possibilities of change as well.[11]

Although, given its conservative associations, feminists have not explicitly embraced theories of the Background, there is a sense in which a critique of the Background has been the project of feminism since its inception as an oppositional movement. The Background in Western thought has defined women as inferior, incapable of the rationality that constitutes both truth and subjectivity. Feminists have challenged this definition and attempted to alter those Background conceptions. Efforts to define the Background precisely *as* a Background and formulate strategies to change it, however, have been rare. Nancy Hartsock's theory of the feminist standpoint is one such attempt. Like Marx, Hartsock is concerned to explicate the construction of social reality, which she defines as the social reality of patriarchy. She also continues the Marxist tradition of defining the Background as ideology, as opposed to Truth. "A standpoint," Hartsock argues, "carries the connotation that there are some perspectives on society from which, however well-intentioned one may be, the real relations of humans with each other and with the natural world are not visible" (1983c: 117). Her defense of the feminist standpoint rests on her assertion that other perspectives can provide a truer vision.

Several elements of Hartsock's feminist standpoint theory, however, move her away from the ideology/reality duality that she inherits from Marx, and toward a feminist critique of the Background. First, she recognizes along with Marx that "reality" as it is constituted by the ruling class, because it defines what reality "really is," cannot be dismissed as simply false, mere deception (1983c: 118). Because it defines the social world in which we all live, the ruling class's reality provides the structure for our consciousness and our material lives. Second, Hartsock clearly identifies this definition of reality as gendered. What she calls "abstract masculinity" structures the real in a fundamental sense and obscures the viewpoint of women.

In *Money, Sex, and Power* Hartsock opposes abstract masculinity to the "feminist standpoint," a perspective developed from the experience of women. As her thought develops, though, Hartsock realizes that "the experience of women" is not singular, but plural. She thus alters her vision of a singular abstract masculinity opposed to a singular feminist standpoint to one in which women with varying experiences occupy the margins and ruling-class white men define the center (1987). This move is significant. It draws her away from the simple reality/appearance binarism that defines Marx's work, toward a more nuanced approach to the constitution of social reality.

I would like to suggest that what Hartsock calls "abstract masculinity" is very similar to what I am here calling the Background, but that the juxtaposition between abstract masculinity and the feminist standpoint is a counterproductive feminist strategy. Abstract masculinity, as Hartsock herself admits, constitutes the definition of the real, the element in which arguments and thought itself make sense. She claims that abstract masculinity is, in an absolute sense, false, and she juxtaposes it to the truth of women's experience, a truth rooted in the real material conditions of women's lives. But in one sense Hartsock has this characterization backwards. Far from being false, abstract masculinity sets the standards for what constitutes "truth." It follows that we cannot simply counter abstract masculinity with the "truth" of the feminist standpoint. This is so, as Hartsock herself later realizes, because there is more than one "truth" to women's experience. But there is another, profoundly important reason why this juxtaposition will not work: feminist truth does not make sense in the discourse of abstract masculinity. When feminists proclaim their "truth," it comes out sounding like nonsense in the terms of abstract masculinity, which is, of course, precisely what it is in those terms. Hartsock is skipping a step here. We must first alter the criteria of what it makes sense to say before we can proclaim another "truth" and expect it to be heard; we must, in Wittgenstein's metaphor, shift the riverbed of thought.

This missed step is crucial. Feminists can proclaim a truth that radically challenges Background assumptions, that reveals the injustices of patriarchy and calls for its abolition. I argued in the last chapter that such radical arguments can reveal the fundamental liabilities of Background assumptions. In the short run, however, radical arguments fall on deaf ears, because they make no sense in the Background's terms. They are thus all too frequently dismissed as the rantings of fanatics and have little chance of altering Background assumptions. A more effective strategy is to construct arguments that both make sense in terms of the Background and at the same time alter those terms by shifting their meaning. A good illustration of this is a strategy that has a long tradition in contemporary feminism: making strange what appears familiar. One of the defining character-istics of the Background is that it is the taken-for-granted elements in which sense is constituted, rather than consciously applied rules. The first step in changing the Background thus must be to bring it into focus – to look at the familiar, identify it, examine its constituent elements, and explore their implications. This is no mean feat. The Background is, by definition, rarely conceptualized. Gadamer's pre-judice, Wittgenstein's riverbed, Foucault's "unthought," and Hart-sock's abstract masculinity exert their influence precisely because they are not conceptualized, and thus not questioned. Conceptualiz-ing and questioning the Background is a radical act. It reveals the Background to be not the ground of all truth, but the ungrounded ground of this society's particular truth.

The next step in the strategy is to argue that what appears familiar is, from another perspective, strange. The feminist "consciousness raising" movement of the 1960s is a good example of this. Women engaged in consciousness raising were examining elements of the Background – aspects of their lives that they had always taken for granted and certainly had never conceptualized. Their scrutiny of these elements yielded radical results. The Background they uncov-ered was an abstract masculinity that marginalized, trivialized, and erased their thoughts and experiences. Conceptualizing these ele-ments led these women to conclude that they were, from their new feminist perspective, strange. These women looked at everyday prac-tices such as opening doors and ushering women into rooms and found them odd, even demeaning, rather than polite. They ques-tioned the link between childbearing and childrearing that resulted in the suburban isolation of white, middle-class women. And they questioned why women's work in the household did not count as "work" at all.[12]

The best illustration of a feminist theorist who employs this strat-egy is Marilyn Frye. In *The Politics of Reality* (1983) Frye examines elements of the Background that are of particular relevance to women, first bringing them into consciousness and then exposing them as peculiar phenomena, "making them strange." One of these elements is what she calls the "habitual and obligatory sex marking" that characterizes our culture. There is, she points out, great pressure on us to *inform* everyone all the time of our sex (1983: 23). In a brilliant analysis, Frye first makes us see that this is indeed the case, then exposes the practice as a bizarre social custom, and finally reveals that there are deep-seated cultural reasons why this practice exists and continues: "There are reasons... why you should want to know whether the person filling your water glass or your tooth is male or female and why that person wants to know what you are, but those reasons are woven invisibly into the fabric of social structure" (1983: 27).

In an effort to describe how this social structure keeps women in their place, Frye evokes the metaphor of a bird cage. No one woman in our culture embodies all of the cultural stereotypes imposed on women, yet we are all restrained by them. These stereotypes operate like the wires of a bird cage. If you look closely at just one wire, it is impossible to see the other wires and thus impossible to understand why the bird is imprisoned. It is only when you step back and look at all the wires that the reality of the prison and the mechanism of restraint become apparent (1983: 4).

What is particularly valuable about Frye's feminist analysis of the Background is that she takes on the difficult question of how we can resist and even change it in feminist directions. Her basic assumption is that "our conceiving cannot be independent of culture, though it can be critical, resistant or rebellious" (1983: xiii). She clarifies what I see to be the feminist relevance of the Background: that it is both the element in which meaning is constructed and that which we must resist and critique if we are to fly out of the bird cage. In *Willful Virgin* (1992) she defines what she calls the "politics of a situation" in a way that is similar to my definition of the Background:

It is useful for some purposes to think of the politics of a situation as like climate and weather, topology and soil: a multidimensional, multi-leveled temporally extended constantly changing, moving medium, a highly structured and fluid play of powers, which both sustains and threatens all the vital processes of human community existence; a sum of forces and pressures, currents, turbulences and calms, variations of density. (1992: 14)

This definition informs the strategy that Frye formulates for changing the Background. She argues that the Background cannot simply be tinkered with, but that it is also not "beyond us" (1992: 15). For Frye, what feminists are doing, and must continue to do, is to create a "matrix and meaning, a world of sense, a symbolic order" (1992: 7). Essential to her argument, however, is her assertion that this creation is not, and cannot be, *de novo* but, rather, is necessarily embedded in cultural understandings and meanings. She is not claiming that we must uncover the true reality obscured by the ideology of patriarchy. Rather, in a Wittgensteinian move, she argues that the new meanings that feminists create must be defined in terms of words that are already intelligible to us. Women who want to create new meanings work within an existing language, system of imagery, and myths. Thus the "new" vocabulary they create is and must be a reassembly of the old (1992: 99).[13]

Frye is, in her own words, a "seer," one who sees the taken-for-granted elements of the Background, brings them to our attention, and challenges them by presenting them as strange. She assumes, along with the nonfeminist theorists of the Background, that meaning is collectively constructed and that without the Background meaning itself is impossible. But she also assumes with these theorists that the Background is ungrounded, and that the point is not to find the "true" ground of meaning but to shift the riverbed in a different direction. Unfortunately, Frye does not have much to say about how we can go about doing this. She asserts that meaning must be communal – women must make it together. She suggests that we can accomplish this by changing the meaning of words that are already intelligible to us, reassembling them to suit our purposes. And, finally, she tells us that this activity takes courage: we must imagine ourselves as beings capable of making meaning (1983: 80).[14]

Shifting the riverbed

"Grammar is politics by other means" (Haraway 1991: 3).

I have argued that a central element of Wittgenstein's description of the Background is his understanding of how Background assumptions might change. But Wittgenstein is no social reformer. His discussion of shifts in the Background is epistemological speculation, not a blueprint for social action. Foucault's discussion of the Background is more useful in this regard. Although disappointingly vague, his discussion of "counter sciences" and the "insurrection of subjugated knowledges" points to where discursive change might originate. Feminist discourse is a "subjugated knowledge," a "counter science," in Foucault's sense. It is a discourse that creates a new picture of reality, a picture based on the experiences of women, which are invisible in the present picture. The now extensive literature on feminist epistemology elaborates the significance of this new picture of knowledge. What has not been extensively discussed in this literature, however, is how the new picture that emerges from feminist discourse relates to the Background. There has been little discussion of how, in the sense I have developed here, feminists can use language understandably but also subversively in order to change linguistic/social practice.[15]

The exception to this is the work of Donna Haraway. In an impressive array of writings that range from primatology to postmodernism, Haraway constructs a feminist narrative that subverts Background assumptions, transforming meaning in a feminist direction. Perhaps the best illustration of this intention and its relationship to what I have identified as theories of the Background is her image of the cyborg (Haraway 1990) that I discussed in chapter 2. It should be evident from that discussion that Haraway's construction of the cyborg rests on many of the assumptions of the Background theorists. She assumes that our picture of reality is a picture that includes some experiences but excludes others. She also assumes that in order to alter this picture, another picture must be constructed, and that this picture, like the picture it replaces, is political. Her Background assumptions are specifically feminist, however, in that the impetus for her investigation is the fact that the Background renders the experience of women invisible, particularly as an object of scientific study.

Haraway's analysis of the cyborg outlines the key elements of her feminist strategy for altering the Background. Haraway assumes that the picture that feminism constructs must be intelligible in terms of the old picture, even as it transforms it. In describing what she calls "my cyborg myth" she refers to "transgressed boundaries, potent fusions, and dangerous possibilities" (1990: 196). Transgressing boundaries is an activity that makes sense only if boundaries are known and what constitutes a transgression is understood. Haraway also assumes that we cannot "prove" the "truth" of the new picture but, ultimately, can only argue for it. This is reminiscent of Wittgenstein's statement that at the end of reasons comes persuasion.[16]

The depth and power of Haraway's feminist critique of the Background is most clearly revealed in *Primate Visions* (1989). On one level, the book is an analysis of the changing discourse of primatology in the twentieth century. But much more is going on in Haraway's book than a straightforward description. Underlying and informing her analysis are three questions: What is the narrative that primatology tells us about nature, culture, race, and gender? Why is primatology so central to this story? How can this narrative be destabilized in a feminist direction? In the course of answering these questions, Haraway significantly develops her feminist strategy for altering the Background.

Haraway addresses the first question, the structure of the narrative that defines nature, culture, race, and gender in the first sentences of her book: "How are love, power and science intertwined in the construction of nature in the late twentieth century?" and "How do the terrible marks of gender and race enable and constrain love and knowledge in particular cultural traditions, including the modern natural sciences?" (1989: 1). Haraway defines her first order of business as understanding the narrative that shapes our definition of nature. The themes of race, sexuality, gender, nation, family, and class, she asserts, have been written into the body of nature in Western science since the eighteenth century. The next step is to understand that this narrative is a story, not a priori truth. A danger to be avoided, she asserts, is to see race and gender as "prior universal social categories" instead of constructed categories, "world-changing products of specific, but very large and durable histories" (1989: 8).

Informing both these steps of Haraway's analysis is her renunciation of objectivity. The "visualizing narrative 'technology' of this book," she claims, is "never innocent" (1989: 2). Its intention is, in Foucault's sense, to reveal the unthought and, in so doing, to destabilize the narrative that it grounds. But, as in her cyborg myth, Haraway is careful to caution that her goal is not to reveal the "truth" but, rather, to construct another narrative. But why primatology? Why not some other discourse, scientific or otherwise? Haraway's answer is that monkeys and apes have a privileged relation to nature and culture for Western people: they serve as surrogates for "man." Primatology, she argues, is a boundary discipline in several senses. Because it defines the boundary between man and animal, it provides a crucial marker for what we identify as human, as culture rather than nature. It is also a boundary discourse between the scientific and the popular. The discourse of apes and monkeys has become a staple of popular culture. Finally, it is a discourse that negotiates boundaries. In its various manifestations, primatology has redefined the boundaries between nature and culture, sex and gender. It is thus a fruitful place to start for those who, like Haraway, want to renegotiate those boundaries (1989: 1–15).

Much of Haraway's discussion in *Primate Visions* centers on how the discourse of primatology has constructed "nature" and how this discourse has changed in the twentieth century. She focuses on the codes that have informed this discourse. "How," she asks, "do the race, species, gender and science codes work to re-invent nature in the Third World for First World audiences within postcolonial, multinational capitalism?" (1989: 135). The gender code emerges with the prominent role of women in twentieth-century primatology. Women, who are closer to nature, can mediate the nature/culture boundary more readily than can men. They bring chimps into culture from nature. The prominence of women in primatology also impinges on the science code: uncredentialed women scientists are more likely to be sensitive to the mother–infant bonding that is one of the principal objects of scrutiny in primatology. Finally, the race code emerges in the prominent whiteness of the women primatologists. White women can mediate between man and animal in a way that colored women cannot. And, in relation to the white women primatologists, the primates are colored surrogates for all who have been colonized in the name of nature (1989: 135–54).

The story that Haraway tells of the discourse of primatology in the twentieth century centers on the intersection between the changing narrative of "man" and the discourse of the scientific study of primates. In the course of the twentieth century the discourse of "man" has moved from a focus on man's role in the traditional, nuclear family, a discourse rife with racism and sexism, to a discourse of "universal man" explicitly defined in terms of the eradication of sexism and racism. The discourse of primatology has made parallel moves. Primatologists in the 1940s and 1950s found traditional families among the primates they studied and a pronounced pattern of male dominance. Researchers in the 1970s and 1980s found a more egalitarian family structure and evidence of female sexual "choice." Summarizing the parallels between these two discourses, Haraway notes that changes in the discourse of primatology "have been a function of, and have in turn contributed to, major political struggles over the social relations of human reproduction and over the political place of all primate females in nature" (1991: 94). In other words, how we look at primates and what we see is determined by how we look at ourselves.

Haraway's contention that primatology is one of the central elements in the construction of "nature," and that the changing discourse of "man" in society both affects and is affected by the discourse of primatology provides her with an opening to her feminist critique. If primatology is the story we tell about nature, culture, gender, and race, and if that story changes with cultural changes, then destabilizing the patriarchal story, and replacing it with a feminist story, should change cultural attitudes toward women. This is precisely the strategy that Haraway employs in her book. Her theoretical point is that all narrative fields offer the possibility of renegotiation: "All units and actors cohere partially and provisionally, held together by complex material-semiotic-social practices. In the space opened up by such contradictions and multiplicities lies the possibility for reflexive responsibility for the shape of narrative fields" (1989: 172). The reason for focusing specifically on the narrative field of primatology is that its position as a boundary discipline makes it a good place to start constructing a new story about men, women, and humanity:

> In a myriad mundane ways primatology is a practice for the negotiation of the possibility of community of a public world, of rational action. It is the negotiation of the time of origins, the origin of the family, the boundary between self and other, hominid and hominoid, human and animal. Primatology is about the principle of action, mutability, change, energy, about the possibility and constraints of politics. (1989: 284)

Haraway's strategy of destabilization emerges as her analysis progresses. What she calls the shape of narrative fields can be opened up and reshaped by telling another story. But this story must be closely related to the original story, intersecting with it in significant ways, while at the same time departing from it sufficiently to alter its meaning. Two assumptions inform this strategy. First, Haraway argues that the best strategy for feminism is not to counter the "false" story of primatology with the "true" story of feminism, but to tell a different story. She asserts: "Destabilizing the positions in a discursive field and disrupting categories for identification might be a more powerful feminist strategy than 'speaking as a woman'" (1989: 310). Second, Haraway assumes that feminism and primatology are intersecting stories, and that it is precisely this intersection that provides the possibility of change.

> My contention is that the intersection of the narrative fields of primatology and feminism destabilizes the narrative fields that gave rise to

both primatology and feminism, thereby generating the possibility of new stories not strangled by the same logics of appropriation and domination, but also not innocent of the workings of power and desire, including new exclusions. But the intervention must work from within, constrained and enabled by the fields of power and knowledge that make discourse eminently material. (1989: 288)

What unites feminism and primatology is that they are both critical discourses that claim to provide knowledge about gendered social space and sexed bodies. They are thus in a unique position to "warp each other's story fields" and redraw possible knowledge positions (1989: 324).[17]

In *Philosophical Investigations* Wittgenstein sketches in the broadest outline a theory of how the Background might change incrementally over time. In *Primate Visions* Haraway utilizes similar understandings of the Background to present a scenario for change from a feminist perspective. Haraway follows Wittgenstein in arguing that our understanding of our world and the possibility of meaning in that world is a story, an ungrounded ground. It is a story, furthermore, that rests on certain founding assumptions. Thus Wittgenstein refers to the elements in which arguments have their life, the contours of the riverbed through which our form of life flows. Haraway puts flesh on this Wittgensteinian model by focusing on the concept of nature and its development in the discourse of primatology. She shows how changes in the concept of nature in primatology are intimately intertwined with changes in society, particularly in what is deemed "natural" for men and women. This is an illustration of Wittgenstein's understanding of the linkage between language and practice. Both Wittgenstein and Haraway assume that language and practice are two sides of the same coin. Haraway, quite obviously, has more to say about practice than Wittgenstein, but they concur in defining changes in practice in linguistic terms.

Haraway also puts flesh on the Wittgensteinian point that changes are products of shifts in meaning of existing elements of the Background. Like Wittgenstein, she argues that changing the story of the Background, although possible, is necessarily an incremental process. Meanings must be destabilized and altered; they cannot be created *de novo*. This becomes clear in her description of the work of feminist primatologists in *Primate Visions*. The story that feminist primatologists tell conforms to the norms of scientific discourse – it is a *scientific* story. But it is also a destabilizing story that alters the narrative field of primatology and has political overtones. Feminist primatologists contend with nonfeminist primatologists about evidence and its meaning. Their story has the same form as that of their opponents. This is precisely why it is capable of shifting the riverbed.[18]

Conclusion

One of the rallying cries of the contemporary feminist movement has been Audre Lorde's (1981) famous dictum: the master's tools cannot dismantle the master's house. Lorde's dictum expresses a powerful sentiment among feminists: the belief that we must tear down the masculinist establishment that oppresses women. I concur with this sentiment. The institutions of patriarchy have to be radically reshaped if feminism is to achieve its goals. But I question Lorde's strategy. I think it is *only* the master's tools that can dismantle the master's house. Attempting to fashion our own tools is both unfeasible and counterproductive.

There are two principal elements to the argument I have presented here. First, the master's tools, the discourses that constitute the Background, define sense and meaning in our society. They define the parameters of what constitute a sound argument. If feminists cast arguments outside those parameters, we will be (and have been) dismissed as talking nonsense – which is not to say that such arguments *are* nonsense. The Background defines what makes sense in the dominant discourse of society; this is not the same as saying that it defines what is true in an absolute sense. But it does constitute what will be called "true" in our discursive context.

Another way of putting this is that discussions of "true" grounding are irrelevant. Neither the Background nor the feminist reality to which it is opposed is "true" in an ontological sense. The point I am making is not ontological, but epistemological. The fundamental beliefs that constitute the Background give us our world; we cannot step outside them and create a new world out of nothing. What we can do is to work with those beliefs, shifting them in a direction more to our liking.

The second element of my argument is that the Background, the master's tools, is neither monolithic nor static; there is a lot of "give" in it. My discussion has touched on several ways of expressing this point. Wittgenstein talks about shifts in the riverbed, hard propositions becoming fluid, fluid ones becoming hard. Foucault and Haraway talk about the interstices between discourses that allow for slippage and thus the possibility of destabilizing meaning. They argue that meaning is unstable on the margins of discourses, providing an opportunity for redefinition and renegotiation. Yet another way of characterizing this possibility is the strategy of incorporating concepts from one language game into the terms of another. In a broad sense this has been the strategy of women and other marginalized groups seeking social and political equality. The language game of gender relations dictates a subservient role for women. But the language game of political liberalism dictates equality for all human beings. Women have been successful in appropriating the language game of equality to begin to rectify the inequality dictated by the language game of gender relations.

None of these representations appeals to the "truth" of social reality, and none relies on the creation of entirely new discourses or language games. My point is that we already have the tools to dismantle the master's house: they are our own tools. This is not Foucault's point that where there is power, there is resistance. My argument, rather, is that power is flexible, diffuse, disparate. Elements of any regime of power can be rearranged in a way that will displace that power, shift it in another direction. And this can be accomplished without positing an alternative metanarrative of "truth."

In the previous chapter I argued that radical arguments, arguments that violate Background assumptions, can be useful in highlighting the limitations of those assumptions. Although they may not be strategically effective in the short run, they are valuable insofar as they force us to examine our preconceptions. I can now offer a redescription of this argument in light of the analysis of this chapter. A radical argument that has gained notoriety in the feminist community is the assertion that "The personal is political." This seems to be the kind of radical argument I am opposing here. It violates one of the founding assumptions of Western thought: the opposition between the political and the private/personal. Ever since Plato and Aristotle, the political has been defined specifically as the opposite of the private; this opposition has been basic to what politics means for subsequent Western civilizations.

As a strategy for changing Background assumptions, the slogan "The personal is political" has made little headway. It has been rejected outright by the masculinist establishment. Even some feminists have rejected it as too radical. But there is another way to look at the fate of this slogan. Claiming that the personal is political is a version of the strategy I discussed above: making the familiar strange.

We all know that the personal is the antithesis of the political. Particularly in liberal societies, the barrier between the political and the private/personal constitutes the very definition of freedom. But, from a feminist perspective, this familiar fact is strange. It is strange that although the elements of a woman's life defined as "personal" have profound political repercussions, they are excluded from the political sphere. Although women are, in liberal societies, equal to men in the political sphere, their inequality with men in the personal sphere belies that equality, revealing it as a sham. Women's personal/ private inequality to men is thus a political fact; their equality in liberal society is *de jure*, not *de facto*.

Furthermore, although the political/legal community has rejected this slogan, it is nevertheless the case that, since it was coined, a significant number of "personal" elements have been brought into the public sphere through changes in the legal code. Changes in the adjudication of rape, laws against sexual harassment, and, most notably, laws against marital rape are all instances of making the personal political. All these represent aspects of personal life that were formerly beyond the public domain of the law but are now an accepted part of our legal system.

Claiming that the personal is political is about transgressing boundaries. The boundary between the personal and the political is fundamental to our definition of politics. It cannot be dismantled by one radical slogan. But it can be revealed as a boundary – the familiar can be revealed as familiar. It can also be transgressed incrementally; changes in the legal adjudication of personal affairs witness to this. The fate of this slogan, then, is a good illustration of the argument I am constructing here. It has not produced a world in which the boundary between the personal and the political has been obliterated. There is a sense in which we would not know how to live in such a world. But it has produced a renegotiation of the boundaries between these two concepts and the social practices they constitute. It has not produced the radical change it proclaims but, rather, a gradual shift in our Background assumptions. Transgressing boundaries is what feminism is all about. But in order to do this, we need to know what the boundaries are and the points at which they can be transgressed. In the end, we are left with the paradox that the radical goals of feminism can best be achieved through less-than-radical strategies.

What I have here called the third strategy of feminism – the challenge of differences – has proved more difficult to negotiate than the first two strategies. The first and second strategies were, in an epistemological sense, relatively straightforward. Each was grounded in a universal epistemology which dictated a clearly defined method that achieved Truth. The third strategy imposes radically different demands. The paradigm shift it entails calls for a new understanding of difference, method, and truth. Although most postmodern theories illustrate what I define as the new paradigm, few are useful in achieving this new understanding. Most postmoderns deny what I see to be the fundamental element of that challenge: formulating methods and defining truth. My task in the foregoing has been to meet that challenge. This has involved outlining a new methodology for feminist analysis that encompasses both differences and general concepts. It has also involved suggesting strategies by which multiple paths to truth can displace hegemonic discourses in moral theory and epistemology. My goal has been to contribute to the understanding of differences that must necessarily dominate future feminist thought.

Notes

1   The Problem of Difference

1   In *The Ethics of Ambiguity* (1948) de Beauvoir argues that man's [sic] freedom lies in his acceptance of the ambiguity of his situation, specifically that he is at the same time free and determined. In a brief discussion of women she argues that women refuse to break into the realm of freedom because they refuse to accept this ambiguity. It is clear from her account, however, that women must first ascend to the realm of full subjectivity before embracing their ambiguity can be a meaningful injunction. In *The Second Sex* (1972) she shows why this is an impossibility.

2   I am not arguing that there are no exceptions to this pattern, or that "Western thought" is monolithic. Following many twentieth-century thinkers, I am pointing to a pattern of dualistic thinking that has dominated Western philosophy.

3   For an elaboration of this argument see Hekman 1990: 49–54.

4   An interesting transition between de Beauvoir/Firestone and O'Brien is Adrienne Rich's *Of Woman Born* (1976). Although Rich advocates the "repossession of women's bodies" as the avenue to essential change, much of the book is concerned with the negative effects of motherhood for both women and society as a whole. Overall, her strategy is more to bring the experience of motherhood into the realm of rational discourse than to rewrite the rules of that discourse as O'Brien suggests. Perhaps most significantly, she warns that it would be "dangerously simplistic" to fix on women's nurturance as a force that could create a

new human order; this strategy, she argues, will "boomerang" (1976: 283).

5　I challenge this interpretation in Hekman 1995.
6　I am not assuming that the feminist theorists who explore the problem of differences are a monolithic group. I am only assuming that they define the issue of differences as central to feminist theory and attempt to solve the problems it raises. It is significant, however, that a theorist who begins with a question very similar to mine defines three phases of feminist approaches to subjectivity that match my three strategies (Dean 1996). See also James Scott 1990 for a definition of a compatible goal for social theory.
7　Judith Butler does this best by arguing that we must conceive of agency not as the province of the Cartesian subject, but as a discursive product like the other attributes of subjectivity (1990: 147). See also Patricia Mann's (1994) advocacy of a social theory of agency.
8　It is significant that one of the most radical attempts to achieve both these goals, Judith Butler's *Gender Trouble* (1990), generated widespread controversy in the feminist community.
9　See also Nicholson and Seidman 1995.
10　Wendy Brown (1995) articulates this argument very eloquently. It is significant for my argument that Weber also discussed the difficulty of operating in a world without absolutes. See also Seidman 1994.
11　The most famous of these is Linda Alcoff, who offers a compromise between "cultural feminism" and poststructuralism (1988). Alcoff wants to have her cake and eat it too. She wants to retain some aspects of the agentic subject of the modernist tradition while at the same time asserting that this subject is a product of discursive practices.
12　See Barrett and Phillips 1992.
13　See Arbib and Hesse 1986, Haack 1993, and Alcoff 1996 for acute discussions of these problems in epistemology.
14　I qualify this in chapter 3.
15　See especially Nelson 1995 and Anderson 1995. Charlene Seigfried (1996) argues for an approach to feminism specifically rooted in American Pragmatism. I disagree with her thesis and characterize my position as "pragmatism" rather than "Pragmatism" because, like the Pragmatists, Seigfried ultimately appeals to a universal conception of human nature.

2　From Difference to Differences: The Case of Feminist Standpoint Theory

1　An earlier version of this chapter appeared in Hekman 1997.
2　There are recent signs that this trend may be reversing. Nancy Hartsock recently published *Feminist Standpoint Theory Revisited* (1998) and a

special issue of *Women and Politics* (183, 1997) was devoted to the approach.

3 For an early discussion of the problem of difference see Hartsock 1983a. She argues that in our society some empirical differences are reified into an ontologically significant "Difference" by the ruling class. She asserts that feminists should reject this construction of "Difference" and, rather, use empirical differences as sources of creativity and power. I find this to be an insightful and useful discussion of difference that has unfortunately been neglected in current debates.

4 This article was first published in 1974.

5 The articles collected in this book were written between the early 1970s and its publication.

6 In her comments on my 1997 article Smith (1997) continues to maintain this position.

7 See Grant 1993 for a similar critique.

8 See Bordo 1990 for a cogent statement of this problem. I discuss it at length in chapter 3.

9 Bar On (1993) offers an excellent account of the epistemological problems entailed by the claim to epistemic privilege and that of the center/margin dichotomy.

10 It is significant that Hartsock runs into difficulties with the "Other" just as de Beauvoir did.

11 For other recent accounts of standpoint theory see Winant 1987, Aptheker 1989, Stanley and Wise 1990, and Campbell 1994.

12 I take up this question in chapter 5.

13 See also Bar On 1993, Hirschmann 1992.

14 All the commentators on my *Signs* article, "Truth and method" (1997), criticized me for privileging epistemology over politics. I hope to demonstrate here that this criticism is unjustified.

3 A Method for Differences

1 See Flax's (1995) counter to Okin's argument.

2 She clarifies this position in Nussbaum and Glover 1995.

3 This follows only if "epistemology" is defined in strictly modernist terms. Code rejects the term for precisely this reason (1991: 314).

4 A corollary of Nelson's thesis is the rejection of Kuhn's view that scientific paradigms are incommensurable. Against this she asserts that when scientists disagree, they do not disagree about everything – there are basic, commonsense commonalities that link paradigms (1990: 241).

5 Judith Butler also seems to be looking for a middle ground when she argues that we should not just reject claims of universality. It may be possible, she argues, to radically rearticulate the universal, remembering that it is always culturally articulated (1995: 130).

6 Weber's relationship to feminism itself is ambiguous. His wife, Marianne Weber, became president of the German Women's Foundation after Max's death. After women's suffrage, she was elected to the Constituent Assembly. Max Weber viewed the freedom and independence of even married women as an inalienable human right, all the while referring to his wife as "mein liebes Kind" (Roth 1988).

7 For an extended analysis of Weber's ideal type see Hekman 1983.

8 Guy Oakes claims that the methodological issues raised by Weber still dominate the philosophy of social science (1988: 2).

9 Breiner (1996) argues that ideal types play a crucial role in the process of value clarification.

10 For arguments for a value-oriented – even political – interpretation of Weber's methodology see Strong 1994 and Maley 1994. The most extreme version of this interpretation is that of Sheldon Wolin (1994). Wolin argues that Weber's methodology amounts to a type of political theory. He asserts that Weber's work has the effect of showing the researcher that science cannot function without evaluative ideas. Wolin uses Weber's work to draw a parallel between the social-scientific researcher and the politician: both must choose which values to endorse, and in both cases that choice is constitutive of the activity itself. Thus Weber's methodology, Wolin concludes, is a form of political practice, a guide for action.

11 See Warren (1992).

12 Breiner notes that "the fragmentary nature of Weber's theory provides a way for the agent to assemble different logics of action into a social constellation in light of his social and political situation and the historical and cultural situation under scrutiny" (1996: 24).

13 Dorothy Smith's work is the best example of this position. It is worth noting that the work that is frequently cited to debunk the subjectivist position, *Women's Ways of Knowing* (Belenky et al. 1986), consists of much more than subjective descriptions of women's experiences. The authors of this book (and its sequel, Goldberger et al. 1996) "listen" to women with the aid of a carefully developed conceptual scheme and a precisely defined methodology; the conclusions they reach offer generalizations about those experiences.

14 These developments have resulted in disadvantages as well as advantages. Ferraro (1996) argues that domestic violence legislation characterizes women as victims rather than agents. Fine (1992) argues that legal remedies for rape, battery, and sexual harassment may not give women the control that they need.

15 Another important analysis that can profitably be understood in ideal-typical terms is Fraser and Gordon's (1995) work on dependency. The authors analyze how the concept (ideal type) of dependency has changed since preindustrial society and the gendered implications of this change. Their definition of "key words" and their analysis of how changes in

these words produce profound social changes parallels my analysis of the effect of feminist analyses of central ideal types.

16 In her analysis of the concept of gender in feminist theory, Mary Hawkesworth (1997) comes to the opposite conclusion. But it is significant that Hawkesworth uses the same criterion that I employ to judge the utility of the concept: does it advance the cause of women's liberation?

17 See Alcoff 1987, Joan Scott 1994, and Elam 1994 for compatible approaches to feminist theory. For an example of the kind of feminist theory for which I am arguing, see Fraser 1994. Fraser proposes two models, what she calls "thought experiments" (and I call ideal types), to analyze the problems of institutional gender inequity in the welfare state. These ideal types illustrate how different perspectives carve up the world differently. They are also explicitly normative, political, and systemic. See also Z. Eisenstein 1994.

Tangential to my discussion of feminist methodology is an on going discussion in sociology about the possibility of a "postmodern" social science. Several social theorists have argued that a "postmodern sociology" is a contradiction in terms if by sociology we mean a systematizing, generalizing social science (Smart 1990, Hollinger 1994). What we need, these theorists argue, is not a postmodern sociology, but a sociology of postmodernity. What I am attempting to do in this chapter is to define a feminist methodology that is appropriate to a new paradigm of knowledge. I argue that we do need a methodology, but one that departs from the methodology of positivist social science.

4 The Epistemology of Moral Voice: Displacing Hegemony in Moral/Legal Discourse

1 In her subsequent work, however, Gilligan has become more sensitive to the influences of race, class, and ethnicity in the constitution of moral voice (Gilligan et al. 1990; Taylor et al. 1995).

2 I discuss this issue later.

3 For an elaboration of these arguments see Hekman 1995.

4 In *The Moral Theory of Poststructuralism* (1995), Todd May develops a moral theory that rejects the transcendentalism of finding one right answer. Although his project has much in common with mine, he does not deal directly with the question that concerns me here: the interaction of multiple moral discourses within one society.

5 See Hekman 1995 for a discussion of the limitations of contemporary theories of moral relativism.

6 See Hekman 1986.

7 The Canadian practice of sentencing circles and the Mexican reliance on family and community courts are examples (Nadar and Metzger 1963).

8 See Bartlett 1990 for a discussion of feminist legal practices that depart from hegemonic legal discourse. Bartlett argues that we need a way of acknowledging the truth claims of these feminist methods.

9 Bower (1992) argues that family court in California was originally established as an alternative court procedure.

10 See also Z. Eisenstein 1988 and Meyers 1994. One of the more intriguing attempts to mix the hegemonic legal standard with a new approach to difference is found in *Multiculturalism and "The Politics of Recognition"* (Taylor et al. 1992). Taylor argues that the politics of difference rests on a metaphysical belief compatible with liberalism: that all persons are entitled to respect and dignity, and that different cultures and identities are equally worthy of consideration and respect. One way of characterizing multiculturalism is the right to cultural definition because cultural identity is an important personal good that liberal society should recognize. On one level this seems like a neat trick: subsuming multiculturalism under the rubric of liberalism. But a closer look reveals a conflict: the belief that a particular ethnic identity is so constitutive of the individual that it must be legitimated. This flies in the face of the autonomous individual that grounds liberal theory.

11 For another attempt to integrate rights with the different voice, see Rhode 1989.

12 See Code 1992 for an argument against erecting the care voice as "a new monolith." See also Walker 1989, 1991. Connolly (1995) advances another argument for treating difference differently.

13 I elaborate on this argument in Hekman 1995.

5 Backgrounds and Riverbeds: Feminist Reflections

1 An earlier version of this chapter appeared in Hekman 1999.

2 My argument here is consistent with Andrea Nye's thesis that we must change philosophy "At the border" (1995); see also Nye 1987, 1990.

3 Nye (1992) makes this argument as well.

4 I see my efforts here as consistent with Linda Alcoff's (1996) effort to define the paradigm shift in epistemology to what she calls "social epistemology." See also B. Smith 1997.

5 Judith Butler makes this argument in *Gender Trouble* (1990).

6 See Ricketts 1996.

7 See Malcolm 1994.

8 For compatible interpretations of Wittgenstein, see Brill 1995 and Edwards 1982.

9 For a discussion of this transition, see Barrett 1991.

10 For an elaboration of these aspects of Foucault's work, see Hekman 1990.

11 There are various other thinkers I could appeal to in order to make my argument here. One obvious one is Gadamer. Gadamer's understanding of prejudice and its role in making meaning possible is a version of a Background theory. His concept of critical reflection on our prejudices, furthermore, allows for both critique and change. But Gadamer cannot in any way be described as an oppositional thinker (although Kogler (1996) attempts to do so). Rorty is another candidate. Rejecting both the transcendental subject and any metanarrative of truth, Rorty describes change in terms of continual redescriptions. "Lots and lots" of redescriptions, he argues, might cause a new generation to adopt "new scientific equipment or new social institutions" (1989: 9). Although this is consistent with my argument, it is too vague for my feminist purposes.

12 See Elliott 1994 for a Heideggerian interpretation of making the familiar strange. An example often used to make this point is Susan Glaspell's play "Trifles" (1987). Glaspell's story has some elements in common with my argument here. What constitutes "evidence" for the men is contrasted with the "trifles" that the women uncover; finding the "truth" is defined by the men's practices; the women's evidence is not evidence at all, but "trifles." The problem with this example, however, is that any good detective would look for precisely the "trifles" that the women uncovered, and it would be precisely this evidence that would be decisive in a trial.

13 I should note that Frye's use of the term "background" in *The Politics of Reality* is different from the way I am using it here. She defines phallocratic reality as the foreground, women as the background, invisible and unnoticed (1983: 167ff). I agree with this characterization, although I have used the term differently.

14 The work of Mary Daly represents the kind of strategy I am opposing. In a series of books culminating in *Webster's First New Intergalactic Wickedary of the English Language*, with Jane Caputi (1987), Daly has attempted to redefine and, in doing so, valorize words that denigrate women. Her work is radical in a linguistic sense: it forces us to confront the hatred of women embedded in our language. But Daly's approach has two liabilities. First, her method is a form of demolition; she uses words like "castration," "exorcism," "methodicide" to describe it (1973). Second, the Background is composed not just of words, but of narratives. Shifting the riverbed of thought requires telling a different story, a story that is intelligible in terms of the story we have been told, but one that also illuminates its strangeness. We must do more than redefine words; we must construct new narratives.

Judith Butler's work, on the other hand, is consistent with the argument I am offering here. Butler (1990, 1993) develops a feminist strategy for change that calls for the subversive redeployment of existing subject positions, with the aim of destabilizing hegemony. In *Excit-*

able Speech she continues this argument by asserting that if we think in ways that have not yet been legitimized, we can produce new forms of legitimation (1997: 41).

15 See Tanesini 1994 and Ferguson 1984 for similar arguments.

16 Crewe (1997) describes Haraway's method as "transcoding": a complex process of displacement, substitution, and transposition from one discursive code to another.

17 For another attempt to warp a story field, see Haraway 1997.

18 In *Primate Visions* Haraway suggests that science fiction is another means by which feminists can destabilize the narrative of primatology. I disagree with this strategy. I think that the intersection of the narrative fields is crucial to the possibility of change, and that science fiction does not provide sufficient intersection.

References

Alcoff, Linda 1987. Justifying feminist social science. *Hypatia* 2(3): 107–27.
—— 1988. Cultural feminism versus post- structuralism: the identity crisis in feminist theory. *Signs* 13(3): 405–36.
—— 1996. *Real Knowing*. Ithaca, NY: Cornell University Press.
Anderson, Elizabeth 1995. Feminist epistemology: an interpretation and defense. *Hypatia* 10(3): 50–84.
Aptheker, Bettina 1989. *Tapestries of Life: women's work, women's consciousness and the meaning of daily experience.* Amherst: University of Massachusetts Press.
Arbib, Michael and Mary Hesse 1986. *The Construction of Reality.* Cambridge: Cambridge University Press.
Austin, J. L. 1961. A plea for excuses. In *Philosophical Papers*, Oxford: Oxford University Press, 175–204.
Bar On, Bat-Ami 1993. Marginality and epistemic privilege. In Linda Alcoff and Elizabeth Potter (eds), *Feminist Epistemologies*, New York: Routledge, 83–100.
Barrett, Michèle 1991. *The Politics of Truth: from Marx to Foucault.* Cambridge: Polity Press.
Barrett, Michèle and Anne Phillips (eds) 1992. *Destabilizing Theory.* Cambridge: Polity Press; Stanford: Stanford University Press.
Bartlett, Katharine 1990. Feminist legal methods. *Harvard Law Review* 103(4): 829–88.
Belenky, Mary et al. 1986. *Women's Ways of Knowing: the development of self, voice and mind.* New York: Basic Books.
Bologh, Roslyn 1990. *Love or Greatness? Max Weber and Masculine Thinking.* London: Unwin Hyman.

Bordo, Susan 1987. *The Flight to Objectivity*. Albany, NY: SUNY Press.

—— 1990. Feminism, postmodernism, and gender-scepticism. In Linda Nicholson (ed.), *Feminism/Postmodernism*, New York: Routledge, 133–76.

Bower, Lisa 1992. Unsettling "woman": competing subjectivities in no-fault divorce and divorce mediation. In Leslie Goldstein (ed.), *Feminist Jurisprudence: the difference debate*, Lanham, MD: Rowman and Littlefield, 209–230.

Breiner, Peter 1996. *Max Weber and Democratic Politics*. Ithaca, NY: Cornell University Press.

Brill, Susan 1995. *Wittgenstein and Critical Theory: beyond postmodernism and toward descriptive analysis*. Athens: Ohio University Press.

Brown, Wendy 1995. *States of Injury: power and freedom in late modernity*. Princeton, NY: Princeton University Press.

Butler, Judith 1990. *Gender Trouble: feminism and the subversion of identity*. New York: Routledge.

—— 1993. *Bodies That Matter*. New York: Routledge.

—— 1995. For a careful reading. In Seyla Benhabib et al., *Feminist Contentions: a philosophical exchange*, New York: Routledge, 127–43.

—— 1997. *Excitable Speech: a politics of the performative*. New York: Routledge.

Campbell, Richmond 1994. The virtues of feminist empiricism. *Hypatia* 9(1): 90–115.

Card, Claudia 1991. The feistiness of feminism. In Claudia Card (ed.), *Feminist Ethics*, Lawrence: University of Kansas Press, 3–31.

Chodorow, Nancy 1978. *The Reproduction of Mothering: psychoanalysis and the sociology of gender*. Berkeley: University of California Press.

Code, Lorraine 1991. *What Can She Know? Feminist Theory and the Construction of Knowledge*. Ithaca, NY: Cornell University Press.

—— 1992. Who cares? The poverty of objectivism in moral epistemology. *Annals of Scholarship* 9(1–2): 1–17.

—— 1995. *Rhetorical Spaces: essays on gendered locations*. New York: Routledge.

Coles, Romand 1996. Liberity, equality, receptive generosity: neo-Nietzschean reflections on the ethics and politics of coalition. *American Political Science Review* 90(2): 375–88.

Collins, Patricia Hill 1986. Learning from the outsider within: the sociological significance of black feminist thought. *Social Problems* 33(2): 14–32.

—— 1989. The social construction of black feminist thought. *Signs* 14(4): 745–73.

—— 1990. *Black Feminist Thought*. Boston: Unwin Hyman.

Connolly, Willliam 1995. *The Ethos of Pluralization*. Minneapolis: University of Minnesota Press.

Coward, Rosalind and John Ellis 1977. *Language and Materialism: developments in semiology and the theory of the subject.* London: Routledge and Kegan Paul.

Crewe, Jonathan 1997. Transcoding the world: Haraway's postmodernism. *Signs* 22(4): 891–905.

Daly, Mary 1973. *Beyond God the Father: toward a philosophy of women's liberation.* Boston: Beacon Press.

Daly, Mary and Jane Caputi 1987. *Webster's First New Intergalactic Wickedary of the English Language.* Boston: Beacon Press.

De Beauvoir, Simone 1948. *The Ethics of Ambiguity.* New York: Philosophical Library.

—— 1972. *The Second Sex.* Harmondsworth: Penguin.

Dean, Jody 1996. *Solidarity of Strangers: feminism after identity politics.* Berkeley: University of California Press.

Ebert, Teresa 1996. *Ludic Feminism and After.* Ann Arbor: University of Michigan Press.

Edwards, James 1982. *Ethics Without Philosophy: Wittgenstein and the moral life.* Gainesville: University Press of Florida.

Eisenstein, Hester 1980. Introduction. In Hester Eisenstein and Alice Jardine (eds), *The Future of Difference.* Boston: G. K. Hall, pp. xv–xxiv.

Eisenstein, Hester and Alice Jardine (eds) 1980. *The Future of Difference.* Boston: G. K. Hall.

Eisenstein, Z. 1988. *The Female Body and the Law.* Berkely: University of California.

—— 1994. *The Color of Gender: reimagining democracy.* Berkeley: University of California Press.

Elam, Dianne 1994. *Feminism and Deconstruction.* New York: Routledge.

Elliott, Teri 1994. Making strange what had appeared familiar. *Monist* 77(4): 424–33.

Elshtain, Jean Bethke 1981. *Public Man, Private Woman.* Princeton, NY: Princeton University Press.

Ferguson, Kathy 1984. *The Feminist Case Against Bureaucracy.* Philadelphia: Temple University Press.

—— 1993. *The Man Question: visions of subjectivity in feminist theory.* Berkeley: University of California Press.

Ferraro, Kathleen 1996. The dance of dependence: a genealogy of domestic violence discourse. *Hypatia* 11(4): 77–91.

Fine, Michelle 1992. *Disruptive Voices: the possibility of feminist research.* Ann Arbor: University of Michigan Press.

Firestone, Shulamith 1970. *The Dialectic of Sex: the case for feminist revolution.* New York: William Morrow.

Flax, Jane 1983. Political philosophy and the patriarchal unconscious: a psychoanalytic perspective on epistemology and metaphysics. In Sandra Harding and Merrill Hintikka (eds), *Discovering Reality: feminist perspectives on epistemology, metaphysics, methodology, and philosophy of science*, Dordrecht: Reidel, 245–81.

—— 1990. Postmodernism and gender relations in feminist theory. In Linda Nicholson (ed.), *Feminism/Postmodernism*, New York: Routledge, 39–62.

—— 1995. Race/gender and the ethics of difference. *Political Theory* 23(3): 500–10.

Foucault, Michel 1971. *The Order of Things*. New York: Random House.

—— 1980. *Power/Knowledge*. New York: Pantheon Books.

—— 1982. The subject and power. In Hubert Dreyfus and Paul Rabinow, *Michel Foucault: beyond structuralism and hermeneutics*, Chicago: University of Chicago Press, 208–26.

Fraser, Nancy, 1994. After the family wage: gender equity and the welfare state. *Political Theory* 22(4): 591–618.

—— 1995. Pragmatism, feminism and the linguistic turn. In Seyla Benhabib et al., *Feminist Contentions: a philosophical exchange*, New York: Routledge: 157–71.

Fraser, Nancy and Linda Gordon 1995. A genealogy of *dependency*: tracing a keyword of the U.S. welfare state. In Barbara Laslett et al. (eds), *Rethinking the Political*, Chicago: University of Chicago Press, 33–60.

Fraser, Nancy and Linda Nicholson 1990. Social criticism without philosophy: an encounter between feminism and postmodernism. In Linda Nicholson (ed.), *Feminism/Postmodernism*, New York: Routledge, 19–38.

Frye, Marilyn 1983. *The Politics of Reality: essays in feminist theory*. Freedom, CA: Crossing Press.

—— 1992. *Willful Virgin: essays in feminism*. Freedom, CA: Crossing Press.

—— 1996. The necessity of difference: constructing a positive category of women. *Signs* 21(4): 991–1010.

Gadamer, Hans-Georg 1975. *Truth and Method*. New York: Continuum.

Gilligan, Carol 1982. *In a Different Voice*. Cambridge, MA: Harvard University Press.

Gilligan, Carol et al. 1985. Feminist discourse, moral values and the law – a conversation: the 1984 James McCormick Mitchell lecture. *Buffalo Law Review* 34: 11–87.

—— 1990. *Making Connections: the relational worlds of adolescent girls at Emma Willard School*. Cambridge, MA: Harvard University Press.

Glaspell, Susan 1987. *Plays by Susan Glaspell*, ed. C. W. E. Bigsby. Cambridge: Cambridge University Press.

Goldberger, Nancy et al. (eds) 1996. *Knowledge, Difference and Power: essays inspired by women's ways of knowing*. New York: Basic Books.

Gordon, Colin 1988. The soul of the citizen: Max Weber and Michel Foucault on rationality and government. In Sam Whimster and Scott Lash (eds), *Max Weber, Rationality and Modernity*, Sydney: Allen and Unwin, 293–316.

Grant, Judith 1993. *Fundamental Feminism: contesting the core concepts of feminist theory.* New York: Routledge.

Green, B. S. 1988. *Literary Methods and Sociological Theory: case studies of Simmel and Weber.* Chicago: University of Chicago Press.

Gunew, Sneja and Anna Yeatman 1993. Introduction. In Sneja Gunew and Anna Yeatman (eds), *Feminism and the Politics of Difference*, Boulder, CO: Westview, pp. xiii–xxv.

Haack, Susan 1993. *Evidence and Inquiry: towards reconstruction in epistemology.* Cambridge, MA: Blackwell.

Haber, Honi 1994. *Beyond Postmodern Politics: Lyotard, Rorty, Foucault.* New York: Routledge.

Haraway, Donna 1988. Situated knowledges: the science question in feminism and the privilege of partial perspective. *Feminist Studies* 14: 575–99.

—— 1989. *Primate Visions: gender, race, and nature in the world of modern science.* New York: Routledge.

—— 1990. A manifesto for cyborgs: science, technology and socialist feminism in the 1980s. In Linda Nicholson (ed.), *Feminism/Postmodernism*, New York: Routledge, 190–233.

—— 1991. *Simians, Cyborgs and Women: the reinvention of nature.* New York: Routledge.

—— 1997. *Modest-Witness@Second-Millennium. FemaleMan-Meets-Onco-Mouse: feminism and technoscience.* New York: Routledge.

Harding, Sandra 1986. *The Science Question in Feminism.* Ithaca, NY: Cornell University Press.

—— 1991. *Whose Science? Whose Knowledge? Thinking from Women's Lives.* Ithaca, NY: Cornell University Press.

Harding, Sandra and Merrill Hintikka (eds) 1983. *Discovering Reality: feminist perspectives on epistemology, metaphysics, methodology, and the philosophy of science.* Dordrecht: Reidel.

Hartmann, Heidi et al. 1996. Bringing together feminist theory and practice: a collective interview. *Signs* 21(4): 917–51.

Hartsock, Nancy 1981. Fundamental feminism: prospect and perspective. In Charlotte Bunch (ed.), *Building Feminist Theory*, New York: Longman, 32–43.

—— 1983a. Difference and domination in the women's movement: the dialectic of theory and practice. In Amy Swerdlow and Hanna Lessinger (eds), *Class, Race and Sex: the dynamics of control*, Boston: G. K. Hall, 157–72.

—— 1983b. The feminist standpoint: developing the ground for a specifically feminist historical materialism. In Sandra Harding and Merrill Hintikka (eds), *Discovering Reality: feminist perspectives on epistemology, metaphysics, methodology, and the philosophy of science*, Dordrecht: Reidel, 283–310.

—— 1983c. *Money, Sex, and Power.* New York: Longman.

—— 1987. Rethinking modernism: minority vs. majority theories. *Cultural Critique* 7: 187–206.

—— 1989–90. Postmodernism and political change: issues for feminist theory. *Cultural Critique* 14: 15–33.

——1998. *Feminist Standpoint Revisited and Other Essays*. Boulder, CO: Westview.

Hawkesworth, Mary 1997. Confounding gender. *Signs* 22(3): 649–85.

Hekman, Susan 1983. *Weber, the Ideal Type, and Contemporary Social Theory*. Notre Dame, IN: University of Notre Dame Press.

—— 1986. *Hermeneutics and the Sociology of Knowledge*. Notre Dame, IN: Notre Dame University Press.

—— 1990. *Gender and Knowledge: toward a postmodern feminism*. Cambridge: Polity Press; Boston: Northeastern University Press.

——1994. Weber and post-positivist social theory. In Asher Horowitz and Terry Maley (eds), *The Barbarism of Reason*, Toronto: University of Toronto Press, 267–86.

—— 1995. *Moral Voices, Moral Selves: Carol Gilligan and feminist moral theory*. Cambridge: Polity Press; University Park, PA: Penn State Press.

—— 1997. Truth and method: feminist standpoint theory revisited. *Signs* 22(2): 341–65.

—— 1999. Backgrounds and riverbeds: feminist reflections. *Feminist Studies* 25(2).

Held, Virginia 1995. The meshing of care and justice. *Hypatia* 10(2): 128–32.

Hennis, Wilhelm 1988. *Max Weber: essays in reconstruction*. London: Allen and Unwin.

Hirschmann, Nancy 1992. *Rethinking Obligation: a feminist method for political inquiry*. Ithaca, NY: Cornell University Press.

Hollinger, Robert 1994. *Postmodernism and the Social Sciences: a thematic approach*. Thousand Oaks, CA: Sage.

Jaggar, Alison 1983. *Feminist Politics and Human Nature*. Totowa, NJ: Rowman & Allanheld.

Kay, Judith 1994. Politics without human nature? reconstructing a common humanity. *Hypatia* 9(1): 21–52.

Keller, Evelyn Fox 1983. *A Feeling for the Organism*. New York: W. H. Freeman.

Kittay, Eva Feder 1995. Taking dependency seriously: the Family and Medical Leave Act considered in light of the social organization of dependency work and gender equality. *Hypatia* 10(1): 8–29.

Kogler, Hans Herbert 1996. *The Power of Dialogue: critical hermeneutics after Gadamer and Foucault*. Cambridge, MA: MIT Press.

Kohlberg, Lawrence 1984. *The Psychology of Moral Development: essays on moral development*, vol. 2. San Francisco: Harper and Row.

Laclau, Ernesto and Chantal Mouffe 1985. *Hegemony and Socialist Strategy*. London: Verso.

Lloyd, Genevieve 1984. *The Man of Reason: "male" and "female" in western philosophy*. Minneapolis: University of Minnesota Press.

164   *References*

Longino, Helen 1990. *Science as Social Knowledge.* Princeton, NJ: Princeton University Press.

Lorde, Audre 1981. The master's tools will never dismantle the master's house. In Cherrie Moraga and Gloria Anzaldua (eds), *This Bridge Called My Back,* New York: Kitchen Table Press, 98–101.

Malcolm, Norman 1994. *Wittgenstein: a religious point of view?* Ithaca, NY: Cornell University Press.

Maley, Terry 1994. The politics of time: subjectivity and modernity in Max Weber. In Asher Horowitz and Terry Maley (eds), *The Barbarism of Reason: Max Weber and the twilight of Enlightenment,* Toronto: University of Toronto Press, 139–66.

Mann, Patricia S. 1994. *Micro-Politics: agency in a postfeminist era.* Minneapolis: University of Minnesota Press.

Martin, Jane Roland 1994. Methodological essentialism, false difference, and other dangerous traps. *Signs* 19(3): 630–57.

May, Todd 1995. *The Moral Theory of Poststructuralism.* University Park, PA: Penn State Press.

Menkel-Meadow, Carrie 1985. Portia in a different voice: speculations on a women's lawyering process. *Berkeley Women's Law Journal* 1: 39–63.

Meyers, Diana T. 1994. *Subjection and Subjectivity: psychoanalytic feminism and moral philosophy.* New York: Routledge.

Mill, John Stuart [1869] 1971. *On Liberty, Representative Government, and the Subjection of Women.* Oxford: Oxford University Press.

Mill, John Stuart and Harriet Taylor Mill 1970. *Essays on Sex and Equality,* ed. Alice Rossi. Chicago: University of Chicago Press.

Minow, Martha 1990. *Making All the Difference: inclusion, exclusion and American law.* Ithaca, NY: Cornell University Press.

Nadar, Laura and Duane Metzger 1963. Conflict resolution in two Mexican communities. *American Anthropologist* 65: 584–92.

Nelson Lynn Hankinson 1990. *Who Knows? From Quine to a feminist empiricism.* Philadelphia: Temple University Press.

—— 1995. The very idea of a feminist epistemology. *Hypatia* 10(3): 31–49.

Nicholson, Linda 1994. Interpreting Gender. *Signs* 20(1): 79–105.

Nicholson, Linda (ed.) 1990. *Feminism/Postmodernism.* New York: Routledge.

Nicholson, Linda and Steven Seidman (eds) 1995. *Social Postmodernism: beyond identity politics.* New York: Cambridge University Press.

Nussbaum, Martha 1992. Human functioning and social justice: in defense of Aristotelian essentialism. *Political Theory* 20(2): 202–46.

Nussbaum, Martha and Jonathan Glover (eds) 1995. *Women, Culture and Development: a study of human capabilities.* New York: Oxford.

Nye, Andrea 1987. The unity of language. *Hypatia* 2(2): 95–111.

—— 1990. *Words of Power: a feminist reading of the history of logic.* New York: Routledge.

—— 1992. Frege's metaphors. *Hypatia* 7(2): 18–39.

—— 1995. *Philosophy and Feminism: at the border.* New York: Twayne Publishers.

Oakes, Guy 1988. *Weber and Rickert: concept formation in the cultural sciences.* Cambridge, MA: MIT Press.

O'Brien, Mary 1981. *The Politics of Reproduction.* Boston: Routledge and Kegan Paul.

Okin, Susan Moller 1979. *Women in Western Political Thought.* Princeton, NJ: Princeton University Press.

—— 1994. Gender inequality and cultural differences. *Political Theory* 22(1): 5–24.

Parker, Lisa 1995. Beauty and breast implantation: how candidate selection affects autonomy and informed consent. *Hypatia* 10(1): 183–201.

Pateman, Carole 1988. *The Sexual Contract.* Stanford, CA: Stanford University Press.

Reinharz, Shulamith 1992. *Feminst Methods in Social Research.* New York: Oxford University Press.

Rhode, Deborah 1989. *Justice and Gender.* Cambridge, MA: Harvard University Press.

Rich, Adrienne 1976. *Of Woman Born: motherhood as experience and institution.* New York: W. W. Norton.

Ricketts, Thomas 1996. Pictures, logic, and the limits of sense in Wittgenstein's *Tractatus.* In Hans Sluga and David Stern (eds), *The Cambridge Companion to Wittgenstein*, Cambridge: Cambridge University Press, 59–99.

Rorty, Richard 1989. *Contingency, Irony and Solidarity.* New York: Cambridge University Press.

Rose, Hilary 1983. Hand, brain and heart: a feminist epistemology for the natural sciences. *Signs* 9: 73–90.

—— 1986. Women's work: women's knowledge. In Juliet Mitchell and Ann Oakley (eds), *What is Feminism? A Re- examination*, New York: Pantheon, 616–83.

Roth, Guenther 1988. Introduction. In Marianne Weber, *Max Weber: a biography*, trans. Harry Zohn, New Brunswick, NY: Transaction, pp. xv–lx.

Ruddick, Sara 1989. *Maternal Thinking: towards a politics of peace.* Boston: Beacon Press.

Scales, Ann 1986. The emergence of feminist jurisprudence: an essay. *Yale Law Journal* 95: 1373–1403.

Schutz, Alfred 1962. *Collected Papers*, vol. 1, ed. Maurice Natanson. The Hague: Martinus Nijhoff.

—— 1964. *Collected Papers*, vol. 2, ed. Avrid Brodersen. The Hague: Martinus Nijhoff.

—— 1967. *The Phenomenology of the Social World*, trans. George Walsch and Frederick Lehnert. Evanston, IL: Northwestern University Press.

Scott, James 1990. *Domination and the Arts of Resistance: hidden transcripts.* New Haven, CT: Yale University Press.

Scott, Joan 1994. Deconstructing equality-versus-difference: or, the uses of poststructuralist theory for feminism. In Anne Herrmann and Abigail Stewart (eds), *Theorizing Feminism: parallel trends in the humanities and social sciences*, Boulder, CO: Westview, 358–71.

Searle, John 1995. *The Construction of Social Reality*. New York: Free Press.

Seidman, Steven 1994. The end of sociological theory. In Steven Seidman (ed.), *The Postmodern Turn: new perspectives on social theory*, New York: Cambridge University Press, 119–39.

Seigfried, Charlene 1996. *Pragmatism and Feminism: reweaving the social fabric*. Chicago: University of Chicago Press.

Shanley, Mary 1995. Fathers' rights, mothers' wrongs? reflections on unwed fathers' rights and sex equality. *Hypatia* 10(1): 74–103.

Sklar, Judith 1964. *Legalism*. Cambridge, MA: Harvard University Press.

Smart, Barry 1990. Modernity, postmodernity and the present. In Bryan Turner (ed.), *Theories of Modernity and Postmodernity*, Newbury Park, CA: Sage, 14–30.

Smith, Barbara Hernstein 1997. *Belief and Resistance: dynamics of contemporary intellectual controversy*. Cambridge, MA: Harvard University Press.

Smith, Dorothy 1979. A sociology of women. In Julia Sherman and Evelyn Beck (eds), *The Prism of Sex*, Madison: University of Wisconsin Press, 135–87.

—— 1987a. *The Everyday World as Problematic: a feminist sociology*. Boston: Northeastern University Press.

—— 1987b. Women's perspective as a radical critique of sociology. In Sandra Harding (ed.), *Feminism and Methodology*, Bloomington: Indiana University Press, 84–96.

—— 1990a. *The Conceptual Practices of Power: a feminist sociology of knowledge*. Boston: Northeastern University Press.

—— 1990b. *Texts, Facts, and Femininity: exploring relations of ruling*. London: Routledge.

—— 1997. Comments on Hekman's "Truth and Method." *Signs* 22(2): 394–8.

Spelman, Elizabeth 1988. *Inessential Woman*. Boston: Beacon Press.

Stack, Carol 1990. Different voices, different visions: gender, culture and moral reasoning. In Faye Ginsburg and Anna Lowenhaupt Tsing (eds), *Uncertain Terms: negotiating gender in American culture*, Boston: Beacon Press, 19–27.

Stanley, Liz and Sue Wise 1990. Method, methodology and epistemology in feminist research processes. In Liz Stanley (ed.), *Feminist Praxis: research, theory, and epistemology*, London: Routledge, 20–60.

Strong, Tracy 1994. Max Weber and the bourgeoisie. In Asher Horowitz and Terry Maley (eds), *The Barbarism of Reason: Max Weber and the twilight of Enlightenment*, Toronto: University of Toronto Press, 113–38.

Tanesini, Alessandra 1994. Whose language? In Kathleen Lennon and Margaret Whitford (eds), *Knowing the Difference: feminist perspectives in epistemology*, New York: Routledge, 203–16.

Taylor, Charles et al. 1992. *Multiculturalism and "The Politics of Recognition."* Princeton, NJ: Princeton University Press.

Toulmin, Stephen 1958. *The Uses of Argument*. Cambridge: Cambridge University Press.

Trebilcot, Joyce 1988. Dyke methods. *Hypatia* 3(2): 1–13.

Tronto, Joan 1995. Care as a basis for radical political judgments. *Hypatia* 10(2): 141–9.

Turner, Bryan 1988. The rationalization of the body: reflections on modernity and discipline. In Sam Whimster and Scott Lash (eds), *Max Weber, Rationality, and Modernity*, Sydney: Allen and Unwin, 222–41.

—— 1996. *For Weber: essays on the sociology of fate*, 2nd edn. Thousand Oaks, CA: Sage.

Walker, Margaret 1989. Moral understandings: alternative "epistemology" for a feminist ethics. *Hypatia* 4: 15–28.

—— 1991. Partial consideration. *Ethics* 101: 758–74.

Warren, Mark 1992. Max Weber's Nietzschean conception of power. *History of the Human Sciences* 5(3): 19–37.

Weber, Marianne 1988. *Max Weber: a biography*, trans. Harry Zohn. New Brunswick, NJ: Transaction.

Weber, Max 1946. Science as a vocation. In H. H. Gerth and C. Wright Mills (eds), *From Max Weber*, New York: Oxford University Press, 129–56.

—— 1949. *The Methodology of the Social Sciences*. New York: Free Press.

—— 1975. *Roscher and Knies*, trans. Guy Oakes. New York: Free Press.

—— 1977. *Critique of Stammler*, trans. Guy Oakes. New York: Free Press.

—— 1978a. Anti-critical last word on *The Spirit of Capitalism*, trans. Wallace Davis. *American Journal of Sociology* 83(5): 1105–31.

—— 1978b. *Economy and Society*, ed. Guenther Roth and Claus Wittich. Berkeley: University of California Press.

West, Cornel 1994. The new cultural politics of difference. In Steven Seidman (ed.), *The Postmodern Turn: new perspectives on social theory*, New York: Cambridge University Press, 65–81.

Winant, Terry 1987. The feminist standpoint: a matter of language. *Hypatia* 2(1): 123–48.

Winch, Peter 1958. *The Idea of a Social Science and its Relation to Philosophy*. London: Routledge and Kegan Paul.

—— 1972. *Ethics and Action*. London: Routledge and Kegan Paul.

Wittgenstein, Ludwig 1958. *Philosophical Investigations*, trans. G. E. M. Anscombe. New York: Macmillan.

—— 1969. *On Certainty*. New York: Harper and Row.

Wolin, Sheldon 1994. Max Weber: legitimation, method, and the politics of theory. In Asher Horowitz and Terry Maley (eds), *The Barbarism of Reason: Max Weber and the twilight of Enlightenment*, Toronto: University of Toronto Press, 287–309.

Yeatman, Anna 1993. Voice and representation in the politics of difference. In Sneja Gunew and Anna Yeatman (eds), *Feminism and the Politics of Difference*, Boulder, CO: Westview, 228–45.

Young, Iris 1980. Socialist feminism and the limits of dual system theory. *Socialist Review* 10(2–3): 169–88.

—— 1985. Humanism, gynocentrism, and feminist politics. *Women's Studies International Forum* 8(3): 117–83.

—— 1990. *Justice and the Politics of Difference*. Princeton: Princeton University Press.

—— 1994. Gender as seriality: thinking about women as a social collective. *Signs* 19(3): 713–38.

Index